Trevor, and Good luck, and God's blessing on everything you do. I love you Trevor and I will never forget you. I remember my first night at Applewood and I remember that I remember you. I remember amazing I knew there was something amazing about the people there. I learned later that the amazing quality was Jesus. Thank u for being there to help show me the way. You wouldn't be a difference in my life. You'll have my really made a difference in my today life. You'll have my prayers always ♡ always

Stephanie Klaudio

Trevor, megan
have fun at
your New
Church We
Loved you
and Welcomed
you. always
come back

Trevor and Megan,
You guys have
been so awsome and you
will never have any idea of
the extent that God has used
you. It has been truly awsome
to see the passion and craving
that you have for God. To put it
in the most simple terms, God's
beauty shines on your faces. Just like
Moses when he came down from the
mountain with the 10 commandments, his
glory is reflected off of you. I hope
in fact I know, that God is goin____se
you in ways you can't ___   thank
God for your obedien___   you
but more than that, I

Jinny Mack

Trevor, Megan,
Thanks for
always pushing way
to be better and
closer to christ.
God Bless !!!
be praying for
you guys daily
in Him
Hope Klein
Silvis

Trevor thanks
for working
with the
youth you'll
be an inspiration
to your new
group just
like you were
to us & especially
me, we'll have to
go ski biading again
some time soon.
visit soon.

Nick Offord

Trevor,

thank for every thing
I don't know how to explan
everything that you. have
done. we will have to go have
Breakfast soon

Phil
Cleay

Trev & Meg :)
You gays rock! Best of
lack to you in our senior
year. Heve a cool summer!
—Chris

Trevor + Megan,
I remember Cross Point + Chicago. Both were awesome. Thank you for your godly examples + great personality. I have been + will continue to pray for you both! "What are you doing!?" I won't forget you two! You were an awesome leader @ Sports Camp in → Chicago. It was a great experience, you taught me a lot. Stay cool + close to JESUS!

BREAK
THROUGH
Prayer

Your little sis in CHRIST, Ligia

P.S. You're both my → brother + sister!

Trevor-
It has been great growing up with you seeing you grow into what you are today. I am going to miss you & Megan. I know that God is going to do wonderful thing threw you both
        Love Christian

Trevor
Thanks for all.
        -Colins.

Trevor- What can I say I had... I really liked when you... oh Well I whish you the Best. really
        N.

Trevor + Megan,
You guys are going to be a amazing family. I will be praying for you. Always remember how God is the center of everything. I look forward to seeing the drive and development of your marriage.   Love Your brother in Christ Travis

THE SECRET OF RECEIVING WHAT YOU NEED FROM GOD

BREAK THROUGH *Prayer*

JIM CYMBALA

AUTHOR OF THE BEST-SELLING *FRESH WIND, FRESH FIRE*

ZONDERVAN™

GRAND RAPIDS, MICHIGAN 49530 USA

ZONDERVAN™

Breakthrough Prayer
Copyright © 2003 by Jim Cymbala

This title is also available as a Zondervan audio product.
Visit www.zondervan.com/audiopages for more information.

Requests for information should be addressed to:
Zondervan, *Grand Rapids, Michigan 49530*

Library of Congress Cataloging-in-Publication Data

Cymbala, Jim, 1943–
    Breakthrough prayer : the secret of receiving what you need from God /
Jim Cymbala.—1st ed.
      p. cm.
  Includes bibliographical references.
    ISBN 0-310-23626-6
    1. Prayer—Christianity. I. Title.
  BV215.C96 2003
  248.3'2—dc22   2003014645

This edition printed on acid-free paper.

Published in association with the literary agency of Ann Spangler and Company, 1420 Pontiac Road S.E., Grand Rapids, MI 49506.

Interior design by Todd Sprague

Printed in the United States of America

03 04 05 06 07 08 09 /❖ DC/ 10 9 8 7 6 5 4 3 2 1

Contents

Preface

Since I've never had the opportunity to attend seminary, God has regularly used theological books to give me much-needed instruction. Of the more than two thousand volumes that line the shelves of my study, none have meant more to me than books on the subject of prayer. They have proven invaluable to my own spiritual growth because they have driven me both to the Scriptures and to my knees.

When I reach heaven, I will want to meet and thank the saints who wrote the books that so affected my life. People like David Brainerd, E. M. Bounds, Charles Finney, and Samuel Chadwick have an investment in my life although they lived decades and centuries ago. They and others did much more than lay out the principles of prayer. Their writings ignited my faith and inspired me to call on the name of the Lord. Countless breakthroughs in my life and ministry can be traced to God using their writings to help this needy pastor in New York City.

Breakthrough Prayer is aimed at more than outlining the important biblical principle of seeking God's help. It is also about what I call the lost prayers of Scripture—the things we rarely pray for even though God has promised them to all his children. For example, when was the last time you heard others pray for joy or to understand God's timing for their lives? We individuals and our churches all suffer great loss when we fail to ask God for the blessings he wants to give us. The following chapters are written in hopes that no one who reads this book will suffer the tragedy of a life summed up by these words from Scripture: "You do not have, because you do not ask God" (James 4:2).

During my pilgrimage of prayer I have also come across a host of books that "clinically" analyze the subject but fail to draw the heart toward the throne of grace. Although biblically correct in their doctrine, they have fallen short of their purpose. Many also fail to highlight the main pitfalls that most often hinder a spirit of prayer in us. Effective praying depends not just on "what to do," but also on "what never to do" if we want answers from God. By his grace, I pray that this book will instruct, inspire, and assist many in breaking through to a new life of asking and receiving from God.

CHAPTER ONE

BREAK-
THROUGH
Blessings

t was a sweltering night in New York. My wife, Carol, and I along with a handful of others had gathered around the altar of our little church in Brooklyn. As we stood together in that rundown building, tears flowing freely and our voices lifted in prayer, we knew that our struggling church faced problems only God could defeat. If anything was going to change, if the church was ever going to reach its potential, one critical ingredient was absolutely required. We could not live one more day without breaking through to the blessing of God.

But what exactly was this blessing we sought? As the young pastor of that inner-city church, I was beginning to realize that the blessing of God is something very real and tangible. It can change a man's life, transform a neighborhood, invigorate a church, and even alter the course of history. Often it is given to the most unlikely people, like a friend of mine whose life seemed cursed from the start. He is a great example of the difference God can make.

Perched on a hill high above the village of Las Piedras was a house dedicated to the powers of darkness. Inside lived a family that earned its living through practicing sorcery, holding séances, and trafficking with evil spirits. The father, a large man who was feared throughout Puerto Rico, was known as "the Great One." His wife assisted in the work and bore him eighteen children—seventeen sons and a lone daughter. The house on the hill became a favorite lodging place for mediums and spiritualists throughout the island.

One of the children was especially affected by growing up in that house. He feared the sorcery practiced there and resented the lack of attention he felt as one among so many children. He got into trouble early and often. One day his father caught him stealing from his mother's purse. As punishment, the five-year-old was locked in a filthy little pigeon house. The boy tried frantically to escape but only succeeded in exciting the birds, who slammed into his little body as they flew around in the darkness. After his father released him, the boy cried hysterically for several hours. The ordeal caused him repeated nightmares.

This son, out of all the others, seemed marked for evil. When he was eight years old, his mother proclaimed that he was not her son but a "son of Satan, a child of the devil!" When he yelled back in anger, "I hate you!" she merely laughed in his face. He was a cursed child in a house of curses.

The boy grew quickly into an uncontrollable rebel. He tried running away from home on five occasions, and the hatred he felt for his parents turned into contempt for all authority. Unable to deal with their troubled son, his parents sent him to New York City at the age of fifteen. Upon arriving at the airport, he quickly disappeared into the streets for two days. Relatives there eventually enrolled him in school, but he was expelled after repeatedly threatening students, teachers, and the school's principal. Soon after that, he left his relatives' home and took up living on the street in one of the toughest neighborhoods in the city.

The young man's life continued to cycle downward. What else could happen to a kid who had been cursed by his own mother, abused by a father who was a satanic priest, and dedicated to the devil?

Nicky Cruz soon became the warlord of a vicious street gang called the Mau Maus. The smoldering rage inside him found expression in violence, crime, and bloodshed. He was a twisted psychopath who frightened even his friends. (A police psychiatrist told him after an evaluation that he was on a fast track to the electric chair.)

Then one day God sent a street preacher, named David Wilkerson, who dared to proclaim the gospel of Jesus Christ to him. Incredibly, the gang leader surrendered his life to Christ. The change was instantaneous. Instead of being full of tortured, self-destructive rage, the young man became filled with love and compassion for hopeless cases—kids like him who seemed bent on destroying themselves.

Before long, Nicky began attending a Bible school in California, where he met his future wife. Later, Nicky returned to Puerto Rico and witnessed the conversion of his mother. Over time, the Lord opened doors all over the world for him to share his story, and he became one of the greatest evangelists of his generation. Untold thousands of people have been led to Christ by this man once dedicated to the devil. Today his four daughters and their husbands and children are all serving the Lord.

The curse on Nicky Cruz was real, but God's blessing canceled the curse.[1]

Unlike Nicky, Carol and I had been believers since childhood, but we were still desperate for God's blessing. Our breakthrough began in that sticky, uncomfortable, old church during a Tuesday night when a handful of believers were crying out in prayer. The Lord would indeed bless us beyond our wildest imagination, using us to reach out to thousands of broken people—drug addicts, drunks, homeless people, and criminals as well as many professional people who also desperately needed to experience God's blessing. Surprises were coming straight from God in heaven, and the surprises continue to this day.

BLESSING THE PEOPLE

Although God has richly blessed us over the years in some dramatic ways, I'm convinced that the kinds of blessings we enjoy are intended for every church and every believer who earnestly prays for them.

In the Bible we see, first of all, that God's blessing is a reflection of his incredible love for his creation. While it is invisible in its essence, his blessing is invincible, overcoming everything that earth or hell can throw against it. This blessing is rooted in the ancient instructions God gave to Moses to be carried out by the high priest of Israel:

> The LORD said to Moses, "Tell Aaron and his sons, 'This is how you are to bless the Israelites. Say to them: "The LORD *bless* you and keep you; the LORD make his face shine upon you and be gracious to you; the LORD turn his face toward you and give you peace."' So they will put my name on the Israelites, and *I will bless them*" (Numbers 6:22–27).

This practice of conferring a priestly blessing in the name of the Lord is what separated Israel from the people around them for all the centuries of its history. Only God's covenant people enjoyed the divine blessing. A nation favored and protected by the Lord, they knew that God had promised to listen to their prayers and be attentive to their problems. The God of the universe had turned his face toward them so that they could receive his supernatural grace. What a privilege to live under the Lord's favor, to daily experience his blessing! What enemy could intimidate them when God was with them in power?

> God's blessing is a reflection of his incredible love for his creation.

The good news is that God is still a blessing God. In fact, the Bible could be characterized as a book revealing the Lord's intense desire to bless every man and woman he has created.

If this surprises you, you have only to consider the fact that love *always* desires to bless the object of its affection.

I'm reminded of this every Christmas Eve as our family gathers to celebrate. Whenever we get together, I'm not thinking about what gifts I might receive. Like most parents and grandparents, that's the last thing on my mind. Instead, I'm thinking about my children and grandchildren, watching as they open the gift-wrapped boxes Carol and I have prepared for them. My joy comes from giving, not from receiving.

Ask yourself whom you most enjoy giving to. That will tell you whom you really love. Self-centered folks find their greatest delight in spending money on themselves, but when you love someone else, your heart is always going out to bless and help them.

This explains why the Hebrew word *barak* and its derivatives are used more than 330 times in the Old Testament. It's the word for "bless" or "blessing," a word first mentioned in Genesis 1:22 regarding the creatures of the sea: "God blessed them and said, 'Be fruitful and increase in number and fill the water in the seas.'" If God desired to bless crabs and tuna, just think of his interest in helping you and me, creatures who are made in his image! In fact, the very first words recorded after the Lord created Adam and Eve are these: "God *blessed* them" (Genesis 1:28).

God's blessing was also the secret behind Noah's escape from the flood. Scripture tells us that "God *blessed* Noah and his sons" (Genesis 9:1). The divine blessing also enabled them to face the daunting task of leaving their ark of safety and starting over. God blessed them first of all by delivering them from judgment and then by providing for them and making them fruitful as they built a new life together.

Like Noah, what stands out about every man and woman God uses for his glory is that they have the special favor of heaven resting upon them. The best words any of us could ever hope to hear from God are the same ones he spoke to Abraham: "I will make you into a great nation [that is, something beyond yourself] and I will bless you" (Genesis 12:2). There it is in its simplest form. God wanted to change Abraham into a great nation, and he wants to change each of us into something more wonderful than we are at present, showering us with his blessings. How could perfect Love ever want anything less for those for whom he gave his Son as a sacrifice for sin?

> God wants to change each of us into something more wonderful than we are at present, showering us with his blessings.

God doesn't just want us merely to enjoy a moderate amount of blessings. He wants to bless us abundantly. How else could the rest of his word to our father Abraham be fulfilled: "and *you will be* a blessing" (Genesis 12:2)? Like Abraham, we bless others when God's favor overflows in our lives so much that it affects the world around us. When that happens, the Lord's name can be praised throughout the earth.

But how can we bless others if we are barely eking out enough power to live our own spiritual lives? How can barren lives ever provide help for those who are searching for life and rest? One of the most important questions we face as Christians in the twenty-first century is the question of whether or not we are really living under the full blessing of God.

UNBLOCKING THE BLESSING

According to Scripture, God's blessing can rest on both men and women, because with God there is no gender bias. His blessing can rest on a family, a child, or even unborn offspring. It can prosper a local church in such measure that an entire city or region will feel the effect of God's favor on that congregation. God's blessing can rest on the labor of our hands, our personal finances, or our physical well-being. In fact, Moses told the Israelites that "the LORD your God will *bless you in everything you do*" (Deuteronomy 15:18). Think of the vast potential we have if we live under the blessing of God!

But then again, the blessing of God does *not* automatically rest on every person, family, or church. Some of us live out our years under a closed heaven. Because God doesn't smile on our lives, nothing seems to work as we struggle on year after year. This can be true even for those who have professed faith in Jesus Christ as Savior.

Likewise, Christian churches can live outside God's favor, becoming like the congregation at Laodicea that Christ warned us about: "So, because you are lukewarm—neither hot nor cold—I am about to spit you out of my mouth" (Revelation 3:16). Doesn't exactly sound as if God's blessings were overflowing in that church! Just because "God is love" doesn't mean that all is well with everyone here on planet earth. In fact, it's possible to live life under God's displeasure, even to the point of bringing his curse down upon us. The Word of God speaks clearly about this subject as something that requires sober thought and honest investigation.

Perhaps no one in the history of Israel treasured the blessing of God as much as David, Israel's second and greatest king. Over and again, David proved the maxim that when the Lord's favor is on a man, he triumphs over his enemies no matter how many or how fierce. No wonder David penned this glorious promise: "They may curse, *but you will bless*" (Psalm 109:28). He was saying that God's blessing is invincible against all the powers of earth and hell.

Many of the new believers at the Brooklyn Tabernacle have come from countries filled with witchcraft and voodoo. These precious souls will sometimes make an appointment to see me or one of the associate pastors. Some are concerned about a former friend or disgruntled family member who is practicing voodoo against them. A sweet lady once nervously related to me that a witch who lived in her apartment building had placed a dead chicken in front of her door as part of a curse against her! You might be amazed to learn that such things still happen in this day and age, but thank God that we needn't fear them when we are protected by the shield the Lord has put around us. What God blesses, no demon in hell can curse.

How reassuring it is to know that no sorcery can undo the *sure* blessings of our Lord. There is no better illustration of this truth in the Bible than the story of Balak, king of Moab, and the mysterious prophet named Balaam. King Balak could see that God was with Israel as this numerous

people moved toward the Promised Land. Realizing an
army could not succeed against them, Balak decided to
implement a more spiritual strategy by hiring a prophet
named Balaam to curse Israel. This proved unsuccessful in
the end, but Balaam's inspired prophecy in response to
Balak's request merits our careful consideration.

> Then Balaam uttered his oracle:
>
> "Balak brought me from Aram,
>   the king of Moab from the eastern mountains.
> 'Come,' he said, 'curse Jacob for me;
>   come, denounce Israel.'
> How can I curse
>   those whom God has not cursed?
> How can I denounce
>   those whom the LORD has not denounced?"...
> "Arise, Balak, and listen;
>   hear me, son of Zippor.
> God is not a man, that he should lie,
>   nor a son of man, that he should change his mind.
> Does he speak and then not act?
>   Does he promise and not fulfill?
> I have received a command to bless;
>   he has blessed, and I cannot change it....
> "There is no sorcery against Jacob,
>   no divination against Israel.
> It will now be said of Jacob
>   and of Israel, 'See what God has done!'"
>   (Numbers 23:7–8, 18–20, 23)

In truth, nothing can overcome the blessing of God on
our lives even though he permits us to face battles along
the way. Even the permitted hardships and conflicts we

endure against the enemy are part of his plan to bless us. But we need to learn to see them in this more spiritual light. While the Old Testament speaks much about outward, physical blessings from God, the New Testament explores the more important, invisible spiritual blessings that we have in Jesus Christ. These are the blessings that bring us joy and peace, preparing us for eternity with our Lord. But both kinds of blessings are far more important than most of us can imagine.

Remember the last part of Balaam's prophecy about the people of God: "It will now be said of Jacob and of Israel, *'See what God has done!'*" (Numbers 23:23). The Lord cherishes his people, and out of that love flows his desire to bless them. It is through these unmistakable blessings that others can witness God's goodness and declare, "Look what the Lord has done!" This is the divine strategy for spreading the message of God's greatness and the salvation he offers to mankind. As his blessings overflow into our lives, we become a living display of what only the Lord can accomplish here on earth.

> Nothing can overcome the blessing of God on our lives even though he permits us to face battles along the way. Even the hardships and conflicts we endure are part of his plan to bless us.

A Christian filled with peace and joy stands out like a light in a day dominated by fear and depression. Such a person proves that God is greater than the worst kind of terrorist threats or economic uncertainties. A man or woman living under an open heaven is more influential than someone who merely spouts theological arguments with no living reality behind them. Even one local church richly blessed by the Holy Spirit accomplishes more for the kingdom of God than twenty congregations living in spiritual barrenness. Nothing, in fact, can replace the blessing of God upon his people. All the human talent, cleverness, and church-growth methods in the world can never compare with the invisible but very real blessing of God.

> I would rather live under God's special favor than anything else in the world! The greatest epitaph we can have on our tombstones is simply this: *"He was blessed by God in all he did."*

The church itself was born nearly two thousand years ago by the blessing of God. Even though the early believers had very few of the advantages we boast of, "the Lord's hand was with them" (Acts 11:21). God's blessing overcame every problem so that the gospel message spread everywhere in power. Because of that, I would rather live under God's special favor than anything else in the world! How else will my preaching make a difference in people's lives? How else can the Brooklyn Tabernacle reach the multitudes living in the emptiness of sin all around it? The greatest epitaph any of us could have on our tombstones is simply this: *"He was blessed by God in all he did."*

THE FIRST SECRET OF BLESSING

What can we do to receive this kind of blessing from God? Is there a secret, and if so, what is it? Fortunately, there are clear biblical directions to guide us. The first obvious instruction from the Lord is that we are *to ask in prayer* for an outpouring of God's favor. You remember what made Jabez stand out in his generation: "Jabez cried out to the God of Israel, 'Oh, that you would bless me ...!'" (1 Chronicles 4:10). Jabez, it seems, could not accept the idea of living *without* the blessing of God. Please notice the emphatic words, "Jabez *cried out*." His was no mere mental prayer, but the deep cry of a soul that could not live without an open heaven above him.

Jabez's prayer reminds us of Jacob, one of the patriarchs of Israel, who also had a breakthrough time of prayer with God one day. One night Jacob wrestled with God-in-the-form-of-a-man and afterward uttered a sentence that has inspired many people throughout the centuries to fervently seek God for more. As the man sought to leave, Jacob responded, "I will not let you go *unless you bless me*"(Genesis 32:26).

This kind of passionate, desperate prayer is definitely out of vogue today. Maybe that's the reason we experience so little divine blessing on both the church as a whole and her individual members. So often we seem content with the status quo rather than reaching out for more of God. Because of this, we seem to have little effect on the world around us. The sad truth is that most of our churches experience relatively few conversions. Instead, we grieve over large numbers of wayward children, a growing tide of divorce, and increased addiction to pornography. All these afflict the church itself—yet even this host of ills can't seem to stir us up enough so that we cry out to God, even wrestling with him if necessary, to secure supernatural help from heaven.

Everywhere I travel, I keep hearing the defensive teaching that fervent, heartfelt prayer is really overrated and not necessary today. Since God is love, some people reason, we just have to ask once and politely for what we need and everything will turn out fine. No need today for prayer meetings and prolonged times of waiting on the Lord, no sir. No need for anyone to persevere in prayer until the answer comes. No, that's part of an old-fashioned, out-of-date theology that belongs to another era.

Well, I have two questions in response to all that:
1. What do these words from the Bible mean?

And the Lord said, "Listen to what the unjust judge says. And will not God bring about justice for his chosen ones, *who cry out to him day and night?*" (Luke 18:6–7).

During the days of Jesus' life on earth, he offered up prayers and petitions with *loud cries and tears* to the one who could save him from death, and he was heard because of his reverent submission" (Hebrews 5:7).

> If Jesus himself prayed with "loud cries and tears" at times, then we can certainly feel free and unashamed to pour out our souls to God.

I do not fully understand the mysteries of how a sovereign God answers the petitions of frail human beings, but it does seem clear that effective praying often involves more than just saying the right words. Seeking God with our whole heart is the kind of Bible praying that secures not just answers but the blessing of God that we all need. If Jesus Christ himself prayed with "loud cries and tears" at times, then I can certainly feel free and unashamed in pouring out my own soul to God. And so can you.

2. When it comes to de-emphasizing prayer and the prayer meeting in churches across the land, where are the spiritual results that prove we have found a better way? I understand all the warnings about emotionalism and the importance of sound Bible exposition. But show me any place where the blessing of God is resting on churches in such fullness that large numbers of people are coming under conviction of sin and turning to the Lord in repentance and faith. Isn't that what we all want to see? Isn't that the blessing of God we so sorely need?

We might need to listen to some of the great souls who have gone before us in the faith, who experienced visitations of God's blessing that shook whole communities. One of the illustrious names from that number is David Brainerd, a great missionary to Native Americans in the 1740s before America became a nation. Though faced with severe obstacles (including an interpreter who was often drunk), this young missionary prayed for both personal revival and a great harvest of souls. His journal has inspired countless thousands of people to pray and surrender their lives in service to God.

> Monday, April 19 [1742]. I set apart this day for fasting and prayer to God for his grace and for him to prepare me for the work of the ministry. I asked him to give me divine help and direct me in preparing for that great work and to send me into his harvest in his own time.
>
> In the afternoon, God was with me in a special way. Oh, how I enjoyed blessed communion with him! God

enabled me so to agonize in prayer until I was quite wet with perspiration although I was in a cool place. My soul was greatly burdened for the world and for the multitudes of souls needing salvation. I think I interceded more for sinners than for the children of God although I felt as if I could spend the rest of my life praying for both. I enjoyed great sweetness in communion with my dear Savior. I think I never felt such an entire separation from this world and more totally surrendered to God. Oh, that I may always trust in and live for my God! Amen.[2]

THE SECOND SECRET OF BLESSING

Another vital channel of blessing comes from God's precious Word, the Bible. I read a certain passage from Revelation many times over before I came to understand its critical significance: "*Blessed* is the one who reads the words of this prophecy, and *blessed* are those who hear it and take to heart what is written in it" (Revelation 1:3). Though this is the introductory passage to the book of Revelation, I believe this promise of blessing is a valid promise that applies to every line of Scripture. A tremendous blessing awaits each of us every day in the Word of God! When we read with a sincere desire to hear God and take his truth to heart by faith, we will receive favor from him.

Think of all the blessings we squander by allowing ourselves to become too busy to spend time with God's Word. Though some believers are in such a woeful backslidden state that they have lost all desire for the Bible, many people want to read it but simply can't find the time. Yet it's more than just a matter of time. Reading the Bible on a regular basis involves engaging in spiritual warfare, because Satan doesn't want us to read it. He knows God intends to bless us through the Bible, so he tries to make us think we are too busy. God helps us to defeat him and his crafty strategies to keep us from the blessing that God wants to give us every day as we come into contact with his Word.

Why not ask God today for fresh grace to read the Bible daily? No matter how many times you have failed, request God's help so that a new love relationship will begin between you and the Word of God. Don't let the devil rob you of the blessing the Lord has set before you! Remember, there is real blessing from the Almighty in reading and taking to heart every inspired word of Scripture.

THE THIRD SECRET OF BLESSING

Perhaps the most critical key in opening a channel for the blessing of God is the one we often find the most difficult: the matter of *obedience through faith*. Obedience, of course, is a first principle of spiritual life in Christ: "For surely, O LORD, you *bless the righteous;* you surround them with your favor as with a shield" (Psalm 5:12).

Who are these righteous people who are surrounded and protected by the blessing of God against every weapon and attack of the enemy? They can't be people who are morally perfect, for there are no such people. No, God's blessing is reserved for those who long with all their souls to walk in his light and holiness. The righteous in this context are those who will not tolerate sin in their lives but who are always quick to confess their disobedience and seek mercy from the Lord.

On who else could a holy God pour out his blessings but on those who "hunger and thirst for righteousness" (Matthew 5:6)? Can our heavenly Father shower us with blessings if we cling to and practice the same sins that nailed Jesus Christ to the cross? Will we experience his favor if we continually grieve the Holy Spirit he has given to live within us? Such a thing is an absolute impossibility in the moral universe that God rules over.

That's why King Saul was rejected by the Lord and David put in his place. That's the explanation behind the story of Esau's losing his birthright to Jacob and the blessing of God along with it. That's why men and women can enjoy the favor of God for decades, only to lose it—and sometimes their ministries—because sin has become so entrenched in their hearts. To lose this blessing because we prefer to cling to our sins is to suffer the most profound tragedy imaginable.

> God's blessings come with unchangeable conditions that have their foundation in his holy nature.

When God gives his holy commands and issues his personal orders for our lives, it is never because he wants to rain on our parade or spoil our party. Motivated always by love, he wants to keep us under the fountain of his innumerable blessings. He wants to freely give more than we want to receive. But his blessings come with unchangeable conditions and requirements that have their foundation in his holy nature.

God wants us to trust him totally by giving him the reins of our lives. This is why he told his chosen one, Isaac,

"Stay in this land for a while, and I will be with you and will *bless* you" (Genesis 26:3). Because Isaac remained where God told him to, the Lord upheld his part of the bargain, smiling down on Isaac's submission and obedience. Even beyond the moral commands of the Bible, God often gives us personal directions so we can stay in the center of his will. How could I make unilateral decisions, without consulting the Lord, and then expect his hand of blessing to follow everywhere *I* want to go?

To obey or disobey? This is the struggle so many of us lose, forfeiting as a result many of the good things the Lord intends. When God clearly reveals a certain path for us to follow, it can become a critical point of obedience upon which hang the blessings of tomorrow. When a remnant of the Jewish people returned to Jerusalem from captivity, the prophets boldly announced that God had made their return possible so that the temple could be rebuilt. Therefore he pronounced a blessing on them the same day they obediently laid the temple foundation: "From *this day* on I will *bless* you" (Haggai 2:19).

The day of obedience became the day of blessing, the moment when God manifested again his bountiful provision for his people. Barrenness was replaced by fruitfulness because the people yielded to God's call on their lives. It's the same today! God is waiting for us to obey by faith the leadings and promptings he so often gives us. As we obey, untold divine resources and grace will be provided. Let us make today the day of blessing, one in which we have a new sense of God's strong hand resting on us.

THE FOURTH SECRET OF BLESSING

There is one more secret to obtaining God's blessing. When Moses was giving his final instructions and farewell address to the Israelites, he gave specific instructions about something called "the third-year tithe." Unlike the regular tithe, or ten percent annual offering, the third-year tithe was reserved for a different purpose.

> At the end of every three years, bring all the tithes of that year's produce and store it in your towns, so that the Levites (who have no allotment or inheritance of their own) and the *aliens, the fatherless and the widows* who live in your towns may come and eat and be satisfied, *and so that the LORD your God may bless you* in all the work of your hands (Deuteronomy 14:28–29).

It is important to see what God is doing here. Every third year, the towns of Israel became huge storage centers for the tithes of this agricultural nation. These offerings were not brought to the place where the Lord was worshiped in Jerusalem, but rather were given to supply the needs of the priests from the tribe of Levi, who supervised the official worship. Levites were not allowed to own land and have their own farms, so God insisted that the people provide for them in a special way.

But that was not all. The third-year tithe was also earmarked for the aliens, orphans, and widows who lived in the community. What was so special about these people that they were to receive the same consideration as the priests? For one thing, aliens were often excluded by others, sometimes becoming victims of discrimination. Orphans and widows were also vulnerable and in danger of all kinds of exploitation. Because of these unfortunate facts of life, even among God's people, the third-year tithe was reserved for them.

What a marvelous, compassionate God we have! He always has a special place in his heart for the vulnerable, weak, brokenhearted, and rejected among his people. This provision was especially touching because aliens were not even part of the chosen people of Israel. Yet the Lord looked out for them! Compassion and concern for the downtrodden, then, is not merely part of a "liberal agenda," but is rooted in the very heart of our Creator.

However, there was even more to the third-year tithe than supplying the needs of Levites, aliens, orphans, and widows. Israel was to give generously "so that the LORD your God may *bless* you in all the work of your hands." It seems that the act of joyfully giving to others actually opened up the windows of heaven so that the people themselves could be blessed.

God still wants to do extraordinary things for followers who imitate him in compassionate giving. How many blessings have we missed out on through stinginess and having a "me-first" attitude? How much more might we receive if compassion and openhandedness characterized our daily living? What a profound and far-reaching truth the Lord revealed to the apostle Paul when he taught that "it is more *blessed* to give than to receive" (Acts 20:35).

> Can we honestly say God is smiling on our life and labor? If not, why not? After all, the problem is never on the Lord's side.

Can you and I honestly say God is smiling on our life and labor? If not, why not? After all, the problem is never on the Lord's side. God wants us to seek his blessings diligently, for "he rewards those who earnestly seek him" (Hebrews 11:6). Whenever we experience his fullness, God's name is honored. He wants us to align ourselves with his own holy character by walking "in the light, as he is in the light" (1 John 1:7). He desires to give liberally to us as we learn to have the same attitude toward others.

WHEN GOD IS WITH YOU

Earlier I told the story of a hopeless kid from Puerto Rico whose life seemed cursed until God got a hold of him. My friendship with Nicky Cruz has shown me just how powerful the blessing of God can be.

Several years ago, Nicky and I were working together on an evangelistic crusade in the capital city of Lima, Peru. More than ninety members of our church had come with us to do street work and sing gospel music in the plazas, where crowds would gather to listen. It was a great way to spread the gospel as well as to advertise the evening rallies in the national stadium where Nicky would be speaking.

Everything went well until the day before the crusade. Newspaper, radio, and TV reporters had gathered for a press conference at a ballroom in the Lima Sheraton. I sat next to Nicky at the head table while a translator filled me in on what was being said.

The questions seemed routine enough until one of the reporters stood up and challenged Nicky: "Why do we need a Puerto Rican from the United States to come here and preach to us about the solution to youth violence and drug problems? Who are you, anyway? Isn't the United States the place where most drugs are used, and don't you have enough problems there to work on?"

The room grew suddenly quiet as the man went on in a voice filled with disdain and hostility.

"We in Peru need a former Puerto Rican gang leader to tell us about God? I resent you even being here in our country!"

Next to me, the translator seemed agitated and began praying under her breath. You could feel the tension in the room as all eyes turned toward Nicky, waiting for his response. There were cameras and open microphones everywhere.

"Thank you very much for your honest question," he began. "Let me tell you a little about my life. *I used to like to hurt people.* I got my kicks from messing up people pretty bad. In fact, *I used to like hurt people just like you.*"

What? Where was Nicky heading? I started praying hard!

"But that was a long time ago, before Jesus changed my life. I didn't come here as an American or as a Puerto Rican, but as a Christian who has been changed by the power of God! You're right, America is a messed up place in many ways, but that's why I leave my wife and four daughters and travel so that people there can hear about the love of Jesus. You live in a beautiful country, but Peru needs Christ just like the rest of the world. And because Jesus changed me from a wild, hate-filled, violent animal on the streets, I want you to know about his power, too."

As Nicky finished, the reporter left his seat and started walking toward the head table. Cameramen drew near to film whatever was about to happen next. *What if the guy throws a punch?* I wondered. *What will Nicky do?*

None of us could have guessed what happened next. Stopping squarely in front of Nicky, the reporter extended his hand, a smile on his face.

"Your answer tells me you are an honest man. I will be there tomorrow night to hear you speak." With that, the two men shook hands, and the rest of us sighed our relief.

How an unschooled man like Nicky, raised in the mean streets of Brooklyn, could defuse such a tense situation with perfect poise and wisdom is a testimony to the blessing of God. When the hand of the Lord is with someone, no dilemma is without a divine solution. The same God who has blessed and used Nicky Cruz to help others is able to do the same for you.

CHAPTER TWO

GOD GOES
with You

Although the world has made giant strides in comprehending subjects like atomic energy and nuclear fusion, most of us still live with only the slightest understanding of the most ancient, dynamic source of power there is—the power that comes from prayer. In fact, we have not yet begun to experience the infinite power and possibility that becomes available when we call on the name of the Lord in prayer. Only as we break through in prayer will we discover what the Almighty can accomplish for us.

To illustrate the incredible potential of prayer, I want to tell two true stories—one from the pages of the Bible and the other the remarkable story of a man I know.

A DESPERATE PRAYER

The book of Judges records a dark period in Israel's history. Though God had given the land of Canaan to them exactly as promised, the Israelites repeatedly turned their back on his instructions, failing to fully possess the land as he had ordered. Instead of driving out the Canaanites, the Israelites intermarried with them. It wasn't long before they began worshiping Canaan's false idols, a practice God had solemnly warned against.

> After Ehud died, the Israelites once again did evil in the eyes of the LORD. So the LORD sold them into the hands of Jabin, a king of Canaan, who reigned in Hazor. The commander of his army was Sisera. . . . Because he had nine hundred iron chariots and had cruelly oppressed the Israelites for twenty years, they cried to the LORD for help (Judges 4:1–3).

Even though the Israelites were God's covenant people, he could not overlook their disobedience. So he imposed judgment and discipline. Political analysts of the day might have explained the national turn of events this way: "Because of King Jabin's superior strength and the outstanding military leadership of his general, Sisera, who commands nine hundred iron chariots, Jabin has been able to dominate Israel and continues to oppress them." While on the surface the facts outlined were true, the analysts would have missed the spiritual reality underlying the entire chain of events. God was behind the whole thing, allowing the Israelites to suffer the consequence of their wrong relationship with him.

For twenty years this oppression continued unabated. This meant that none of Israel's young people had ever tasted freedom. Exploitation and hardship was a way of life for everyone—until one special day something changed.

That's when, in utter desperation, Israel decided to call on the name of the Lord. Their prayer was the beginning of a breakthrough that changed everything, as we will see.

A DESPERATE MAN

Now fast forward with me to a deserted street in the Bronx at three o'clock in the morning. We are right outside a New York City hospital. A forty-four-year-old man lies in the gutter waiting for the hospital to open. He is waiting, not to get well, but to die. His 108-pound body is covered with sores. A muttering, half-mad creature filled with phobias that paralyze him, he has lived in the streets for three years. His head is filled with voices that scream incessantly, voices he has been speaking to for some time now. The dominant voice hurls constant accusations at him while another voice spews out a steady stream of profanity.

Danny Velasco is someone you cross the street to avoid. He is pitiful and hopeless, a homeless heroin addict ready to die. And that's what he wants, but not there in the street. Danny is hoping to hold out until morning so he can die in a hospital in the Bronx.

Danny's early years gave no hint that he would end up in such a state. He was a normal, well-adjusted kid with a younger brother and two stepsisters, a kid who knew he had a talent for something. In his case, his talent was for styling hair. In fact, his sisters made the perfect practice subjects, letting him experiment on them as he tried out different cuts and styles. Like all aspiring artists, Danny knew that practice makes perfect. Once he accidentally glued his sister's eyes closed while trying to apply false eyelashes!

Let Danny tell you the rest of his amazing story:

"When I was age seventeen, I was hired by Bergdorf-Goodman's, the exclusive department store on Fifty-Seventh Street near Fifth Avenue. I was the youngest hairdresser and makeup artist in the store's history. It wasn't long before I styled the hair of a model who was then photographed by *Seventeen* magazine. From then on I was determined to have my artistry showcased by the most beautiful women in the world, captured on film by the most gifted photographers working with the best lighting people. That way my talent could be exposed to the whole world. Perhaps I fit the definition of an egomaniac, but that was what drove me to excel.

"Curiously, at the same time, I struggled with a very strong inferiority complex. I felt like 'two people,' filled to the brim with energy and ambition while being afraid and insecure. This inner tug of war erupted on a day when I least expected it. I was twenty-one and traveling around the country conducting seminars for other hairdressers when I experienced a devastating panic-attack. Immediately I consulted a doctor, who prescribed Valium. It seemed like such an easy solution. Unfortunately, I found that Valium went down best with large doses of vodka. Soon I was drunk nightly but able somehow to function during the day.

"By my late twenties my career had stagnated. Feeling restless, I decided to move to Paris, so I could jump-start things. Although I arrived in the fashion capital with no portfolio for prospective employers, doors suddenly opened and things exploded for me almost overnight. My work appeared on the cover of dozens of fashion magazines. I had a gorgeous apartment in Paris; and I was earning tons of money—I had reached the pinnacle of my profession.

"Four years later, I returned to New York as someone in tremendous demand within the industry. Having earned my ticket to stardom, I could easily make $3,000 a day working on beautiful models from around the world. The envy of everyone in my profession, I rented a 5,000-square-foot loft in the city. But what no one knew was that I had brought something else back from Paris with me—an addiction to heroin.

"Getting heroin in Paris was one thing, but copping drugs in New York City meant going to the street. So here I was, a successful hairdresser and makeup artist by day, but a drug fiend by night. Most nights I would dress 'down,' roaming the streets of the Lower East Side, and it wasn't long before arrests and missing work became a problem. I was two people at the same time, enjoying euphoric highs and suffering devastating lows, traveling with celebrities on private jets and staying in plush hotels. But that artificial bubble ended every time I returned home. I was empty and miserable no matter where I found myself.

"One day a beautiful redheaded model on a photo shoot began to talk to me about God. *What do I know about God?* I thought. So I let her go on talking. She asked me to do some private work on the side, cutting hair for her and some friends, and she also invited me to visit her church. I didn't mind making a few extra dollars, but the church thing was out of the question. Danny Velasco and church did not go together as far as I was concerned. I definitely was not buying the 'God business.'

"Later I went to Wanda's apartment and styled her and her roommate's hair. Before I left, Wanda asked if they could pray for me. I agreed, never dreaming they meant to pray there and then! They also prayed very loud, as if God could actually hear what they were saying. This freaked me out a bit, but Wanda said, 'Danny, the day you call on the name of the Lord, you will be set free.'

> "Danny Velasco and church did not go together as far as I was concerned. I definitely was not buying the 'God business.'"

"Whatever she meant, I knew it would never happen to me. I had already been in and out of eight or nine detox programs, and nothing had worked. No way any of this 'miracle stuff' could change me! Once a dope fiend, always a dope fiend, I reasoned. If that's the way you lived, then that's the way you died. My life was hopeless and I knew it. I continued to see Wanda regularly in the workplace, and she kept telling me about Jesus. She was sweet, but a real 'fanatic.'

"On a photo shoot in the Caribbean, things started getting totally out of control. I overdosed out on a boat and the Coast Guard had to be called in to evacuate me for medical treatment. When you get to that level in the fashion industry and something happens so publicly, it doesn't take long for word to get out that you're a mess-up and an insurance risk. Production coordinators would even supply drugs if you could keep working, but overdosing was something else.

"My career didn't fade. Instead, it nose-dived straight into the ground. I went from making thousands of dollars a day to nothing. Credit problems mounted, although I shuffled my many debts with all the credit-card tricks I knew. When your rent is $4,000 a month, it doesn't take long to get into deep trouble.

"Then one day I couldn't take the pressure any longer. I took my driver's license, passport, credit cards, and every other form of ID I had and cut them into pieces. Then I walked out of my apartment and began to live on the street. At that point I had no friends and didn't even have a quarter to my name. Each morning I would awake drug-sick, caring only about two questions that faced me: Where would I get my drugs that day, and what would I have to do to get the money to buy them? That's how I lived for the next three years.

"One day I called my agent collect from a pay phone. She told me that someone named Wanda was trying to reach me. When I returned the call, Wanda asked if I could come over to cut hair for her and a few friends. I agreed, but told her things were a little tight. Could she possibly advance me some money before I came over the next day? Wanda wanted to help, but said I'd have to meet her at the Brooklyn Tabernacle, her church, since she'd be there for the Friday night choir practice.

"Dirty as I was, I showed up at the church, and Wanda handed me the money inside a Bible! I used the money for drugs and sold the Bible within an hour of leaving the church. But while I was there, Wanda introduced me to a girl named Roberta, who supposedly had been strung out on drugs herself. *No way,* I thought. *She looks too happy and healthy.*

"When I arrived at Wanda's place the next day, she had five other fanatical Christians waiting to have their hair done. I realize now that it was a Holy Ghost ambush. Before I left, they circled around me, praying so hard it made me think, *Wow, they really believe in this stuff! And there's five of them on me now!* I didn't believe in whatever nonsense they were into, so I left as soon as I could and returned to the street.

"After that my phobias only got worse, and I began suffering from anxiety attacks that literally immobilized me. Then the voices started. At first I heard a few speaking to me in my head. Before long, they were screaming at me incessantly. I became like an animal in the street, muttering or yelling out a stream of profanity as people passed by. By then I looked like a skeleton, covered with sores and abscesses. I had contracted hepatitis A, B, and C, and by the time I reached that hospital in the Bronx, I couldn't even stand up straight.

"I realize now that it was a Holy Ghost ambush. They were praying so hard it made me think, *Wow, they really believe in this stuff!*"

"That particular hospital closed down during the night. I only hoped the staff would let me in to die a decent death, because I didn't want to die in the street.

"Finally the doors opened, and I was admitted and someone gave me an injection that knocked me out. When I woke up, I found myself in a bed, covered in my own vomit. Suddenly all the voices in my head started screaming, creating total chaos within me. I was so disoriented, I wanted to die! But I couldn't jump out a window because they were barred.

"Then, in the midst of all my pain, something or someone whispered words I had heard before: *The day you call on the Lord, he will set you free.* All the other voices tried to drown it out, but they couldn't! I don't know if it was an angel or the Holy Spirit, but the words came through clearly: 'The day you call on the Lord, he will set you free.' In absolute desperation I screamed from my bed, 'Jesus, help me! O God, help me with everything! You're my only hope, so please help, Jesus!' I didn't understand anything about prayer, so I even used 'personal references' as I cried out: 'Jesus, Wanda said that when I called on your name, you would deliver me. So help me now, O God.'

"At that moment Almighty God swept over me and around me. I knew he was real because all the voices in my head suddenly stopped their hellish screaming and the ball of fear that had been weighing on me lifted. I knew everything had changed even though nothing outwardly had— I was still lying in my vomit in a hospital bed in the Bronx. But I was a million miles from where I had been before I said that prayer. The day I called on the name of the Lord Jesus Christ, he did set me free!"

Danny Velasco went from that hospital in the Bronx to a three-month rehab program. In short order, he gained thirty-five pounds and his body began to heal. From there he eventually ended up in a Christian program in upstate New York, where he devoured the Bible like a man ravenous with spiritual hunger. He loved reading the New Testament, because that's where he could get to know this Jesus who had set him free.

In the eight years since his conversion, Danny's spiritual growth has been strong and steady. He has wonderful compassion for people who are hurting and shows a gift for public speaking and ministry. It's exciting to see how the Lord is using this "hopeless case" of a man to show the world the depth of his grace and power.

It's exciting to see how the Lord is using this "hopeless case" of a man to show the world the depth of his grace and power.

Today Danny also belongs to the Brooklyn Tabernacle Choir and sings in two services each Sunday. Who can imagine the joy he feels whenever the choir members lift their voices and sing one of his favorite songs, "God Is Still Doing Great Things"! Great things, indeed!

OUR BREAKTHROUGH GOD

Many people would consider the supernatural change in Danny Velasco's life an astonishing answer to prayer. But this is exactly what the Lord has promised in response to our prayers. We too easily forget the truth of what the angel told Mary: *"For nothing is impossible with God"* (Luke 1:37). Still, not all answers from God come in the same package. The Israelites and their struggle against their Canaanite oppressors offer a classic example of this principle.

God was about to break Israel's twenty-year bondage because his people had finally humbled themselves and begun to cry out for his help. But his solution may not have been exactly what they had been praying for. No doubt they would have liked God to annihilate the enemy army and its nine hundred iron chariots immediately. Instead, the Lord sent a prophetic word to Deborah, who was the judge, or leader, of Israel at the time. Under the inspiration of the Spirit of God, Deborah delivered a message to a man named Barak:

> "The LORD, the God of Israel, commands you: '*Go*, take with you ten thousand men of Naphtali and Zebulun and *lead the way* to Mount Tabor. I will lure Sisera, the commander of Jabin's army, with his chariots and his troops to the Kishon River and *give him into your hands*'" (Judges 4:6–7).

Many of us can only imagine one specific method for God to answer our prayer:

1. We have a need.
2. We ask for God's help.
3. He sends the answer we ask for.

While God often does work in this manner, he also responds in more complex ways. That's what happened with the Israelites in this case. God's answer came in the form of a call to courageous action on the part of God's people. Barak was ordered to go forward and lead an army of 10,000 men to meet the enemy face-to-face. God could have slain all of Sisera's army in their camp, but instead he summoned his people into a cooperative endeavor with him.

Barak's response to Deborah's challenge forms one of the more amusing incidents in Scripture. With less than robust faith, he replied: "If you go with me, I will go; but if you don't go with me, I won't go" (v. 8). Barak didn't exactly follow in the dynamic footsteps of Abraham and Moses. God himself had promised to be with him, but he wouldn't budge unless Deborah held his hand.

> God could have slain all of Sisera's army in their camp, but instead he summoned his people into a cooperative endeavor with him.

So Deborah went with Barak, and Barak marshaled his troops into position on Mount Tabor. When Sisera heard of this development, he led his forces into battle position opposite them. Now the stage was set for the Lord to do as he had promised in answer to the prayer of his people.

> Then Deborah said to Barak, "Go! This is the day the LORD has given Sisera into your hands. Has not the LORD gone ahead of you?" (v. 14).

The pivotal day had come that would end twenty miserable years of servitude to the Canaanites. Notice that God said he had already "given" (past perfect tense) the enemy into the hands of Barak. Still, it was incumbent on Barak and his forces to *go* as the Lord commanded. God would fight for them only as they fought the enemy themselves. As it often is, the promise of God was conditioned on the obedient response of his servant.

Think of some of the responses Deborah's prophecy could have generated today. Some of us might have wanted to conduct an extended praise-and-worship service right there on Mount Tabor to celebrate the phenomenal things God had said through Deborah's prophetic word. But deliverance and victory were not possible as long as Barak stayed on that mountain. The Word of God is clear on the matter: *"At Barak's advance,* the LORD routed Sisera and all his chariots and army by the sword" (v. 15). When exactly did the Lord route the enemy? It was when Barak and his troops moved down the mountain in obedience and faith that God upheld his part of the bargain. There's definitely a time for worship, but it's not when God has ordered a full-scale assault on the enemy!

Others might have pointed out that the Lord is sovereign and omnipotent, so why think that mere human beings have to do anything to secure God's victory? "Stay up on the mountain, Barak, God doesn't need you fighting the Canaanite army." This kind of thinking is biblically false and a cause of spiritual barrenness in both individual believers and local congregations. Israel would never have thrown off the yoke of the Canaanites if saddled with such theology.

This is why Paul ordered Timothy to "do the work of an evangelist" (2 Timothy 4:5) even though it could mean risking your life back then. Prayer for conversion is important, and it is true that only God can save a soul. But unless his servants boldly proclaim the gospel, how will the kingdom of God be extended?

How does the story of Barak apply to us? Often God will give us victory—if we step out in faith to do our part. We have to obey his directions. Could it be that we sometimes fail to receive God's best because we remain passive when he is summoning us to act in cooperation with his purposes? Have we oversimplified our theology to the point where we never listen for directions from the Lord?

Thank God for the faithful response of Barak and his troops! Instead of sitting around on Mount Tabor discussing thorny theological issues, they arose, risking their lives as they swept down the slopes to face the enemy. We need a lot more Baraks today who will break through in prayer and then obey God's leading so that cruel captivities can be overturned. Sometimes prayer involves petition combined with much watching and waiting in faith to secure the answer. At other times, calling on the Lord results in a call to action so that he can work through us. We need the Holy Spirit's teaching in regard to prayer and receiving answers from God!

> Often God will give us victory—if we step out in faith to do our part. We have to obey his directions.

But some people were missing from Barak's army when it swept down the mountain to victory. The "Song of Deborah," the portion of Scripture that ends this section of the book of Judges, mentions those who drew back among the campfires with much "searching of heart" instead of joining the battle (Judges 5:16). The Lord rebuked these noncombatants through Deborah's prophetic song—which surely must have been accompanied by somber chords, for how else could such words be put to music?

"Curse Meroz," said the angel of the LORD.
   "Curse its people bitterly,
because they did not come to help the LORD,
   to help the LORD against the mighty" (Judges 5:23).

Nowhere else in the Bible does the angel of the Lord use such ominous language. It seems God was deeply angered by those who sat out the war while their fellow countrymen risked life and limb to fight on his side. Instead of the blessings usually associated with an appearance of "the angel of the Lord," a curse was proclaimed.

These people were not indicted for something they did, but for something they didn't do. They did not "help the LORD." Those who disregarded the Lord's answer to their prayer came under the most fearful judgment.

Does Almighty God really need our help? Of course not. But when the Lord's method for accomplishing his purpose includes you and me, then it is both a wonderful privilege and a sacred responsibility for us to respond with faith. When Danny Velasco first called on the name of the Lord, God sent immediate mercy and grace to help him in his time of need. His story serves as a reminder of the awesome power of a prayer-answering God!

Even so, the next prayer Danny prays might be answered in a totally different manner. It may involve being recruited to attempt something he never imagined he could do. If that happens, the Lord will have gone before him and the outcome will be secure. The same is true for you and me as we serve the Lord.

Don't be afraid to ask God for great things. Anything less dishonors the One who has given us such awesome promises. When his answers and blessings come showering down upon us, let's praise him with all our hearts. But on those occasions when he whispers, "Go! Arise, and do what I've shown you to do," let us remember that many of the sweetest answers to prayer involve working together with God to accomplish his purposes.

CHAPTER THREE

CALLING
911

*I*magine waking in the middle of the night to the noise of an intruder seeking to break in. You lie still, frozen with fear. A telephone sits just a few feet away on a nightstand. All you need do is pick up the phone and dial 911, and the police will respond instantly. But what if you're from another country and know nothing of our emergency procedures? Or what if panic freezes your mind? The right call at the crucial moment could save your life. But you have to pick up the phone.

We have the same kind of "911" access to God, but our direct line to the throne of grace will do us little good if we fail to use it. Throughout the Bible we see how victories were won and negative circumstances overcome when a man or woman prayed the right prayer at the crucial moment. Out of hundreds we could choose from, here is a classic illustration from the pen of the psalmist David:

> Listen to my cry for help,
> my King and my God,
> for to you I pray.
> In the morning, O LORD, you hear my voice;
> in the morning I lay my requests before you
> and wait in expectation (Psalm 5:2–3).

Notice the fervency of David's prayer as he asks God to "listen to my cry for help." This is a matter of desperate pleading, not relaxed prayer, because David was a man who had enemies to contend with. If he were to survive their attacks, he had to have help from heaven. There was no "plan B" lurking in the background. But David didn't need another plan, because he knew whom he was petitioning: "my King and my God," the Lord for whom nothing is impossible.

David is a man who prayed much and received much. In contrast, those who seldom ask receive in proportion to their little faith. Yet David's faith was not in the power of prayer itself but in the God who answers prayer. That is the secret of every man and woman throughout history who has learned firsthand about God's faithfulness—they knew to whom they were praying.

Many Christians have so little faith that they soon buckle under the pressures of life, while others find the grace to live joyfully above the battle even though they face far more daunting circumstances. As I counsel people, I have noticed that the same challenges that bring weariness and bitterness to some seem hardly noticeable to others who simply pray their way through them. Such people are not operating out of a simplistic theology but a revelation of the character of God, who delights to display his faithfulness in answer to prayer.

Too often we fail to avail ourselves of God's help, forgetting to pick up the phone and make the call. When we finally do pray, we find ourselves tongue-tied in the presence of God. After mumbling a few platitudes along with a request or two, we fall strangely silent. Despite our need for help, we find it difficult to say what is in our hearts. Fortunately, the Bible is full of examples of how God's people approached his throne with their petitions, pouring out their hearts before him. Such examples can instruct our own prayer life as we begin to understand the awesome privilege of coming to the throne of grace.

PRAYING FOR MERCY

Whether or not we know it, all of us are engaged in spiritual warfare daily. To prevail against the devices of Satan, it is vital that we understand one thing especially: God shows mercy in answer to prayer.

King Solomon must have known this, because on the day the temple in Jerusalem was dedicated, he lifted his hands to heaven and prayed this remarkable prayer:

> Hear the supplication of your servant and of your people Israel *when they pray* toward this place. Hear from heaven, your dwelling place, and when you hear, forgive (1 Kings 8:30).

Knowing the waywardness of God's people, Solomon wanted to make certain that mercy would always be available to them. He knew that approaching a holy God always requires that we put away sin, so he asked God to hear and forgive *whenever* the people prayed to him. What a comforting and invaluable truth this is: God forgives our sins whenever we call on him for mercy!

Why is this truth so important when it comes to battling the enemy? Because Satan is called "the accuser of our brothers"—and sisters (Revelation 12:10). One of his most effective strategies is to use our sins as a tool to bring us into guilt and condemnation. But God's grace is far greater than our failures. It doesn't matter how terrible our offenses or how often we've failed—God blots out every sin when we sincerely ask for mercy. This promise is even more precious for us because we live after the most important event in history: the death of Christ on the cross. "If we confess our sins, he is faithful and just and will forgive us our sins and purify us from all unrighteousness" (1 John 1:9).

> To prevail against the devices of Satan, it is vital that we understand one thing especially: God shows mercy in answer to prayer.

As in every facet of prayer, a request for mercy must come from a sincere, repentant heart that hungers for righteousness:

> If my people, who are called by my name, will *humble* themselves and *pray* and *seek my face* and *turn* from their wicked ways, then will I hear from heaven and will forgive their sin and will heal their land (2 Chronicles 7:14).

Notice that this summons to pray with a clean heart is not addressed to France, Argentina, Nigeria, or the United

States of America. It is directed to "my people," which meant Israel in the Old Testament and which now means all Christians on earth. It is important to remember that God never identifies unbelieving Americans, Nigerians, Mexicans, or anyone else as "my people."

This breakthrough praying that brings new blessing from heaven involves humility of heart, fervency of spirit, and a 180-degree turn away from sin. If we secretly plan to continue in our disobedience, the heavens will be like brass above us because God is not only love, but also holy.

When Philip visited Samaria in the early days of the church, a wonderful harvest of souls came to the Lord as a result of his ministry. Among them was a man named Simon, who had earlier made his living by practicing witchcraft. When Simon saw Peter and John laying hands on people and imparting the Holy Spirit, he offered to pay them for the power to do the same. Peter rebuked him:

"May your money perish with you, because you thought you could buy the gift of God with money! . . . *Repent* of this wickedness and *pray to the Lord*. Perhaps he will forgive you for having such a thought in your heart" (Acts 8:20, 22).

We should etch these words in our minds: "Repent of this wickedness and pray to the Lord." Repentance is the only true "deliverance" for Christians who find themselves in the grip of sin. It is the one sure road leading out of darkness into God's sunlight. Blaming our families, our environment, or an evil spirit for our behavior means we miss the point. Peter knew how to cast out demons but that wasn't what Simon needed. Instead, the apostle told Simon to repent and pray to the Lord. This formula, if sincerely followed, is guaranteed by God to break sin's stronghold and bring mercy "running like a prisoner set free, past all my failures to the point of my need!"[1] Until we take responsibility for what we do wrong, we won't find freedom even if Peter and John themselves were to lay hands on us.

I fear that the modern-day "deliverance movement" for Christians has produced a generation of people who never weep over their rebellion against God but who merely wait for the next prayer line or "man of God" to visit town. That doesn't solve anything. In fact, the solution is much simpler: We need to repent and pray, remembering that the God who delights to show mercy is near, waiting for us to call on his name.

> The God who delights to show mercy is near, waiting for us to call on his name.

Sharing our moral failures with others is sometimes both appropriate and beneficial as the apostle James says: "Therefore *confess your sins* to each other and *pray for each other* so that you may be healed" (James 5:16). Sadly, we rarely practice this kind of confession today because of our entrenched self-righteousness and our dislike of being vulnerable. After all, it's humbling to admit to another human being that we have failed God. In some circles Christians rarely ask for prayer for themselves even though the apostle Paul made it a common practice. Our desire to impress others with our spiritual depth often keeps us from experiencing the true victory that God gives in response to prayer. When was the last time you sincerely humbled yourself by asking someone to pray for you?

I recently received a letter from a woman living in the Midwest who described how God had blessed her when she visited one of our services. After the sermon that morning, I did something I often do. I asked people to join with someone nearby in order to pray personally for each other. This woman told me how she had entered the sanctuary that day weighed down by a problem that had troubled her for several weeks. Feeling spiritually fatigued and at her wits' end, she turned to another woman, and they joined hands and began to pray. Suddenly she heard her prayer partner praying boldly and specifically for her, using language exactly describing her dilemma. Since the woman was praying with a total stranger, she knew the Holy Spirit was at work through her partner to help her believe that God knew and cared about her need.

That morning this woman wept for joy, finding fresh grace to surrender her cares to the Lord. What blessings we forfeit when we fail to take God's Word seriously to "pray for each other"! Like this woman, I have been helped by the prayers of other believers, especially at crucial times when Satan has fiercely assaulted me. Let's not allow pride and self-consciousness to rob us of the good things God intends.

PRAYING FOR PERSONAL GUIDANCE

Solomon didn't stop at mercy. He also prayed for wisdom for God's people:

"Then hear from heaven and forgive the sin of your servants, your people Israel. Teach them the right way to live" (1 Kings 8:36).

As Christians we know that the blood of Christ has washed away *yesterday's* sins. But how do we live *today* to please God? Although forgiveness of past failures is wonderful, we still must confront the challenges and complexities facing us each new day. Solomon's prayer implies that there is a teaching by the Holy Spirit that can be had by asking. While the Lord has appointed some in the body to be our teachers, each of us can also benefit from divine instruction. Listen to what Paul says about this:

> Now about brotherly love we do not need to write to you, for you yourselves have been *taught by God* to love each other (1 Thessalonians 4:9).

Let's face it: Life is fraught with choices, some of which are not all that clear-cut. Though the Bible is crystal clear about certain moral principles and doctrines, there are other subtle, yet important issues it does not discuss in detail. What is the best way to rear our children; to relate and witness to non-Christians; to deal with concerns about financial debt, credit cards, and savings; to know God's will concerning a job change or relocation? These and a thousand other questions should make us ask the Lord daily to teach us the right way to live. God has an answer to every challenge we face, and he will reveal it to us as we pray in a childlike fashion. As a Father leads his child by the hand, the Lord will guide us day by day. Our struggle is to slow down long enough to spend time with God to do two things: ask and listen. It helps, of course, if we realize that we're not as smart as we think. We really do need the Holy Spirit's help to navigate through life.

Today prayer for personal guidance is almost a lost art. Our tendency is to run around doing what we think best and *then* ask God to bless our activity. We can learn a lesson from the leaders of Israel who approached the prophet Jeremiah in the midst of a political and military crisis. Their request was simple: "Pray that the LORD your God will tell us *where we should go and what we should do*" (Jeremiah 42:3).

> God has an answer to every challenge we face, and he will reveal it to us as we pray in a childlike fashion.

God's plan for our lives includes the "where" we should go and the "what" we should do. Waiting before him for direction is never a waste of time. As we pray, we will also learn that "less" is often "more" as the Lord guides our steps. Ten words spoken to someone at God's prompting will accomplish more than one hundred of our own. The pastor who preaches a God-directed sermon will feed his congregation the food they need most. If you've ever felt as if you can't take it anymore (and who hasn't), don't give up. Instead, try humbly asking the Lord *where* you should go and *what* you should do.

For years I battled with insecurity about never having attended Bible school or seminary. How could I successfully lead a congregation without instruction in preaching and pastoral techniques? Now, after thirty years of church experience, I have come to a different conclusion. My lack of formal training drove me to pray a thousand times over: "Where should I go?" and "What should I do?" Seminary training is a privilege and blessing, but it fails its purpose if it turns out graduates who don't know how to depend on the leading of the Holy Spirit. I still ask those same questions of God today because I know that I will never outgrow my daily need of his hand guiding me.

BATTLE PRAYERS

Some prayers in the Bible seem obsolete to us. They come from an era in which military battles were an ordinary part of life for God's people. What possible relevance could these petitions have for followers of Jesus? Consider Solomon's prayer:

> "When your people go to war against their enemies, wherever you send them, and *when they pray* to the LORD ... then hear from heaven their *prayer* and their plea, and *uphold their cause*" (1 Kings 8:44–45).

Just as it is today, Israel was surrounded by hostile forces when Solomon was king. Without God's help, the nation could not survive. Israel's armies had to depend on God for success in battle. In his prayer Solomon was rehearsing before the Lord the principle that had applied since the days of the exodus from Egypt: Whenever God led Israel to fight, he would sustain their cause in response to prayer.

Although we live in a vastly different era, as Christians we are still involved in spiritual battles. Consider Paul's words of warning to the Ephesian Christians:

Put on the full armor of God so that you can take your stand against the devil's schemes. For our struggle is not against flesh and blood, but against the rulers, against the authorities, *against* the powers of this dark world and against the spiritual forces of evil in the heavenly realms (Ephesians 6:11–12).

Personal emissaries of Satan war against our souls. Though we must daily fight these invisible powers, God has provided us with spiritual armor—the shield of faith, the helmet of salvation, the breastplate of righteousness, and so on. In addition to describing our battle gear, the apostle Paul gives vital instructions that remind us of Solomon's ancient prayer.

And *pray* in the Spirit on all occasions with *all kinds of prayers* and *requests*. With this in mind, be alert and always *keep on* praying for all the saints (Ephesians 6:18).

Notice the sweeping nature of this admonition: "on *all* occasions . . . with *all* kinds of prayers and requests . . . *always* keep on praying." This need for constant prayer is probably the most overlooked aspect of spiritual warfare. Just as God promised to fight with Israel's armies against its enemies and his, so he promises to uphold our cause as we daily seek his strength. No matter what satanic devices or how many demonic forces are arrayed against us, nothing can match the awesome power of God, who responds to our call for help in the day of battle. The next

> No matter what satanic devices are arrayed against us, nothing can match the awesome power of God, who responds to our call for help in the day of battle.

time you are in the midst of spiritual crisis, consider what Jesus did on the night he was arrested.

> Then Jesus went with his disciples to a place called Gethsemane, and he said to them, "Sit here while I go over there and pray" (Matthew 26:36).

If Jesus, the Son of God, had to pray in order to find strength, what does that mean for us? Think how different your past might have been if in every circumstance and trial you had *always* kept praying, just as Jesus did. I know of a unique ministry whose goal is to restore and encourage pastors and missionaries who have been forced out of the ministry for various moral lapses. I learned an interesting fact gleaned from this organization's interviews with hundreds of clergymen. In not one case was the minister at the time of failure experiencing a daily meaningful prayer life. The problem was not God's refusal to give grace but rather man's refusal to ask God for the strength to withstand sin's onslaught. In the garden of Gethsemane, Jesus cautioned his disciples, as he still cautions us, against the laziness that leads to danger.

> "Watch and pray so that you will not fall into temptation. The spirit is willing, but the body is weak" (Matthew 26:41).

Some temptations are part of everyday living, but others can be avoided if we learn to do two things: become spiritually alert and form the habit of prayer. Earlier in his ministry Jesus had taught his followers to pray, "Lead us not into temptation." Then in Gethsemane, near the end of his life on earth, he reinforced this powerful truth. Real prayer to the living God helps us escape sinful enticements and deadens the seductive pull of others on our souls. The world has yet to see a Christlike, victorious, and fruitful believer who was not a person of considerable prayer. So don't let one day pass without putting on the full armor of God and remem-

> The world has yet to see a Christlike, victorious, fruitful believer who was not a person of considerable prayer.

bering, too, the efficacy of praying "in the Spirit on all occasions with all kinds of prayers and requests."

BREAKING THROUGH TROUBLE

The world is increasing in troubles of every kind. Prospective wars and terrorist attacks, the danger of nuclear and biological weapons, economic woes, and the challenge of rearing children in a hostile and immoral environment are problems we face daily. Surveys show that these difficulties and uncertainties are taking a heavy mental and emotional toll on people. New York City, where I pastor, was already a pretty dangerous place before suffering through 9/11 and the ensuing international tension. What is a Christian to do in the middle of all the uncertainty and trouble? The best place to start is with the promises of God:

> Therefore let everyone who is godly pray to you
>   while you may be found;
> surely when the mighty waters rise,
>   they will not reach him.
> You are my *hiding place;*
>   you will protect me from trouble (Psalm 32:6–7).

The truth is that we live among free moral agents who often choose evil, resulting in inescapable trouble for others. This was what God's people experienced throughout history, from Noah to the apostle John. But although the "mighty waters rise," God is still a "hiding place" for the godly who pray to him in the hour of testing. Instead of complaining, we should recall the simple formula of our Lord's brother, James: "Is any one of you in trouble? He should pray" (James 5:13).

> It doesn't make biblical sense to counsel Christians who have not yet prayed about their "trouble." Who knows what God might do to help such people if only he is given the opportunity?

It doesn't make biblical sense, then, to counsel Christians who have not yet prayed about their "trouble." Who knows what God might do to help such people if only he is given the opportunity? How often do we spin our wheels, talking and worrying, while the Lord of the universe waits to be invited into the fray? This special access to God was what separated Israel from other nations.

> What other nation is so great as to have their gods near them the way the Lord our God is near us whenever we pray to him? (Deuteronomy 4:7).

God's willingness to draw near to those who ask for his help is an overlooked fact of the spiritual life that we desperately need to recover. God performs acts of power in response to prayer that he would not otherwise do. If this is not true, then the Bible is filled with countless inaccuracies and fairy tales.

Remember those annual physicals when the doctor hits your knee with a rubber hammer to check your reflexes? I've always marveled at how my leg instinctively moves upward whenever that certain spot is struck. We need a new spiritual reflex that causes us to pray each time we face trouble. Wouldn't it be better to have a trouble-prayer reflex than the more familiar trouble-worry one? As we follow God's plan for our lives, trouble and danger may well confront us. This is why Paul solicited prayer from other churches:

> *Pray* that I may be rescued from the unbelievers in Judea (Romans 15:31).

> And *pray* that we may be delivered from wicked and evil men, for not everyone has faith (2 Thessalonians 3:2).

The apostle knew that danger was lurking as he preached the gospel, so he asked others to pray on his behalf for both rescue and deliverance. Like Paul, countless Christian missionaries have experienced miraculous help when confronted with trouble brought on by wicked and evil men. Their prayers, joined with the prayers of others, have helped them break through the worst kind of crisis.

Of all the answers to prayer for deliverance and safety, none is more remarkable than that of a young woman named Genelle Guzman-McMillan, whose prayer, whispered from beneath tons of concrete and steel, resulted in an unforgettable story of God's delivering power.

The second youngest of thirteen children, three of whom died in childbirth, Genelle grew up on the Caribbean island of Trinidad. Though her mother was a devout Catholic,

Genelle disliked church, thinking it a waste of time. As the youngest girl in the family, she chafed at living in a house with so many people and so many rules to follow. When she was nineteen and expecting her first child, she moved in with her boyfriend. The relationship lasted for six years. After they split up, Genelle started spending more time at clubs and parties, feeling she was at last coming into her own, living the life she had always wanted. She loved the music, the dancing, and the partying—powerful antidotes for her painful shyness. By then she was also a single mother of two young children. But Genelle didn't mind. She had made it through college and was enjoying life as a single woman with no one to answer to.

Urged by friends and family already in New York, she moved to the city in 1998, planning to bring her children as soon as she could save the money. But that would take time. Meanwhile, New York was a city of endless clubs and parties—a great place for a young woman who loved hanging out and having fun. Later she discovered that her children's father, her ex-boyfriend, wasn't ready to let them leave Trinidad without a fight, and Genelle was not a fighter.

By then Genelle was living with Roger McMillan, a tall man who loved parties and dancing as much as she did. The two had an apartment in a working-class neighborhood in Brooklyn on the day Genelle's life took a remarkable turn.

"I was an office worker assigned to the Tunnels, Bridges, and Terminals Department of the Port Authority of New York. On the morning of September 11, I got to work a little after 8 a.m. After grabbing an egg and a bagel and a cup of hot chocolate, I rode the elevator up to the sixty-fourth floor of the north tower of the World Trade Center, where I had worked for the last nine months. Most of the staff wasn't in yet. I was making small talk with a coworker when it happened. Suddenly the building began to shake. What was that! An earthquake in lower Manhattan? I had no idea that American Airlines Flight 11 had just slammed into the building.

When I looked out the window to see what was going on, I could see bits of paper and debris floating down from above.

"A coworker shouted that a plane had hit the building. I pictured a little private plane, not a jetliner. Because I didn't think we were in any real danger, I was surprised to see people grabbing their stuff and heading for the elevator.

> "Because I didn't think we were in any real danger, I was surprised to see people grabbing their stuff and heading for the elevator."

"One man had already called the Port Authority police downstairs, who assured us things were okay. We should stay put and not leave. I walked over to Rosa Gonzalez's cubicle. She was my closest friend at work. Both of us loved the same things—parties, clubs, and dancing. By now Rosa was in a panic, wanting to leave but confused, feeling she should first call her sister, her daughter, anyone she could think of. I decided to call Roger to tell him I was coming out. He promised to meet me at Century 21, a clothing store across the street. When Rosa and I finally headed out, we discovered the elevators were no longer working. Worse yet, someone had reported smoke on the stairs.

"I didn't know what to do. Should I stay put and wait for help or try to get out? I was too scared to leave on my own, so I decided to stick with the folks who were still on the floor. Whatever they decided, I was going with them. Rosa and I gathered with the only other people who hadn't yet left the Port Authority offices. There were architects and engineers and office workers, people I had seen before but didn't really know—fifteen people in all. Someone had turned on the television in the conference room, and we could see that our building was on fire. Reporters were speculating on a possible terrorist attack.

"Then suddenly the building began swaying and rocking. I couldn't believe it. A second plane had hit the south tower! 'Oh my God,' I said, 'the building is going down!' But one of the engineers, an old man, just kept saying, 'It's not going to fall; it's not going to fall; the building has been designed so it will not fall!'

"Then smoke began pouring into our floor, so someone taped off the lobby doors and the rest of us ran around wetting down sweaters and jackets to block off the doorways and keep the smoke out. By then, only about half the lights on the floor were still working and the smoke was getting thicker. That's when one of the guys, Pasquale Buzelli, said, 'Listen, it's been an hour and no one has come to help us. We've called 911. We've called the Port Authority police. But nothing has happened. We have to leave.' Yet the old engineer refused to budge. 'I'm not going! I was here during the first bombing and got out okay. I'm not moving!'

"Then we heard another huge noise. The building was swaying and shaking again. This time, I was sure we were all going to die. I didn't know that the south tower had just collapsed and that it would only be a matter of minutes before the north tower would go down as well. As soon as things settled, Pasquale and another man removed the tape on the lobby doors and we headed down stairway B. Rosa and I held hands, crying and shaking. The old man who had refused to leave was right behind us. We kept counting the stairs ... 63, 62, 60 ... 50, 49, 48. We could see firefighters headed up the stairs. Some of them had stopped to rest, weighed down by heavy hoses and equipment. They told us to keep going, we'd be all right. By the time we got to the thirtieth floor, I thought they might be right. Then we hit the fifteenth floor. My leather heels were killing my feet. Rosa urged me to stop and take them off, but I didn't want to lose a minute.

"By the thirteenth floor I couldn't take it anymore. As I leaned over to remove my shoes, the whole place just went boom! Everything went completely black. It felt as though something had just hit me in the chest. Rosa and I fell back toward the wall, and then I fell toward the floor. Everything was crumbling around us. It seemed like a dream. I told myself it was. I tried to get up but something hit me and I fell straight to the floor again. By now it was pitch black. I couldn't see a thing. My eyes and mouth were filled with grit and dust. One hundred ten floors were coming down around us. I knew I was being buried alive. The noise was deafening.

"Finally things got quiet, really quiet. I couldn't believe I was still breathing—lying on my right side, with my right leg pinned beneath something. I tried moving my head, but my hair, done up in cornrows, was pinned under the concrete.

"I knew then I was going to die. Nobody was going to find me under all the steel and concrete. I started calling out for Rosa, but there was no response. Then I heard a man saying, 'Help, help, help.' His voice grew fainter, and then there was nothing.

"There in the dark, my mind started racing. I thought of my children, my family, and my fiancé, Roger, who was waiting outside for me. More than anything, I worried about what would happen to me after I died. I didn't know how to ask for forgiveness. I was sure I was going to hell.

> "I knew then I was going to die. Nobody was going to find me under all the steel and concrete."

"I was in and out of consciousness. Every time I woke up, I tried removing the rubble with my left hand, the only part of me that could still move freely. But there was too much. My head was starting to swell, and I wanted so badly to get it free of the concrete, pushing forward and then backward, but the space was too small. That's when I started to pray. 'God, I can't take this pain. Help me get my head free of the concrete.' Then I made one hard pull, yanking upwards. I could feel the cornrows ripping from my scalp. My head was bleeding, but at least it was free.

"As I explored with my free hand, I realized I was trapped under a stairwell. By then my right foot had started to swell, and I could feel iron and steel sticking into my side. I kept trying to remove the rubble, but it was too heavy and hard. Everything was *so* hard. Suddenly my hand brushed against something soft. It was a body. A man's leg. Oddly, it didn't frighten me. I was just glad for the chance to rest against something soft. I fell asleep.

"When I woke again I told myself I had to do something. But what could I do? 'God, you've got to help me!' I prayed. 'You've got to show me a sign, show me a miracle, give me a second chance. Please save my life!' My eyes were so caked with grime that the tears couldn't come, but I felt it in my heart. I was talking to God as though he were right there. I told him I was ready to live my life the right way. 'Lord, just give me a second chance, and I promise I will do your will,' I fell asleep praying the words, and when I woke up I kept praying for a miracle. The more I prayed, the less I thought about the pain in my foot and my side. After a while it got so cold that I knew night had fallen. I was freezing, and still no one had found me.

"The next day I heard a beep-beep sound like a truck backing up. I called for help, but there was no response. I could hear people talking on a walkie-talkie, so I called out again and again. Nothing! Finally someone hollered back: 'Hello, is somebody there?' 'Yes, help me! My name is Genelle, and I'm on the thirteenth floor,' I cried, not realizing how ludicrous the information about my location must have sounded, coming from a pile of rubble.

"The rescue workers shined a light, but I couldn't see it. But I could see a bit of daylight coming through a crack, so I stuck my hand through it. 'Can you see my hand?' I yelled, nearly out of strength. No, they saw nothing. I asked again, stretching my hand as far as I could. But they still couldn't find me. I lost consciousness.

"When I woke, I could hear that my would-be rescuers were above me. 'Please, God, show me a miracle now! Please help me!' I prayed. I tried yelling again, but they still couldn't locate me. So I stretched out my hand as far as I could, and this time someone grabbed it. 'Genelle, I've got you! You're going to be all right. My name is Paul. I won't let go of your hand until they get you out.'

"'Oh, thank God! Finally, someone has found me. Thank you, God!' I tried to see who it was, but my eyes were so encrusted that I couldn't make out a face, though I could feel his hand on mine. As soon as he grabbed my hand, I felt complete calmness throughout my body. Paul kept telling me I would be all right, and I believed him. I kept his name in my head because I wanted to meet him when I got out of there, to thank him.

"I didn't know it then, but I was the last survivor to be pulled out of the wreckage of what had once been the World Trade Towers."

"I could hear men moving steel and concrete above me, trying to get to me. Finally, two men took hold of my shoulders and Paul let go of my hand. They put me on a stretcher and then passed me hand to hand up and down a long line of people. When the sun hit my face, I saw them all lining the path, firemen and workers. Everyone was clapping. It had been twenty-seven hours since the towers collapsed. Of the fifteen of us who had tried to escape, only Pasquale and I had made it out. I didn't know it then, but I was the last survivor to be pulled out of the wreckage of what had once been the World Trade Towers.

"I spent five weeks in Bellevue Hospital and underwent four surgeries on my right leg. But that day I wasn't worried about what lay ahead. I was just happy to be alive, excited to see Roger and my family. It never occurred to me to wonder what I looked like after being buried alive for twenty-seven hours. I was laughing and smiling when I saw my sister, but as soon as she caught sight of me, she broke into tears, and Roger looked so puzzled when he bent down close to my face. He couldn't even recognize me. My sister begged the nurse not to give me a mirror, but I insisted. The face that stared back at me was twice its normal size, with eyes puffy and purple. The skin was covered with abrasions, and the hair, still in cornrows, was caked with white dust. There were two bald spots on either side of my head where I had ripped it free of the concrete. Soon all of us were crying together.

"Roger kept asking me, 'Why didn't you leave when you said you were leaving?' While I was up on the sixty-fourth floor trying to figure out what to do, Roger had been standing outside, frantically asking people what floor they had come from. When a man said he had come from the seventy-seventh floor, he couldn't believe it. Where was Genelle? Why wasn't she out yet? When he saw the second plane hit the building, he felt sick. He knew how fragile I am, that I can't run very fast, can't lift heavy things. The day I went missing, Roger started drinking. He felt so hopeless, he wanted to die.

"It was hard for me to spend so much time in the hospital, because I was impatient to start living the life I had promised Christ I would live when I was buried under all that concrete. I wanted to go to church, to get baptized, to start living the right way so I told Roger we couldn't live together anymore. 'I've given my life to Christ and made a promise and I'm not going to go back on it.'

"My brother-in-law helped me so much during that time. He would visit during his lunch break and read the Bible to me. Then he'd suggest passages I could read on my own. Every day we did a little Bible study together. A lot of other people came and prayed with me, and that comforted me a great deal. My life was very different than it had been before. I was amazed by how much God loved me.

"But the hospital staff still worried about me. They wondered why I didn't seem depressed or fearful. Maybe the enormity of what I had suffered hadn't yet sunk in. Maybe I was repressing feelings I couldn't bear to face. Perhaps I would explode one day, go crazy because of the terrible thing that had happened to me. *Why was I so quiet?* they wondered. *But why shouldn't I be quiet?* I thought. I've always been a shy person. The difference was that now I was peaceful too.

"Every day a psychiatrist would visit me in my hospital room. The man kept badgering me: 'Genelle are you

> "It was hard for me to spend so much time in the hospital, because I was impatient to start living the life I had promised Christ I would live when I was buried under all that concrete."

okay? It takes time to work these things out. I want to help you. Are you having any nightmares?'

"'No, not even one,' I assured him. And to this day, I haven't had one nightmare about September 11.

"Then he started asking questions about my childhood, but what did that have to do with anything? A building had collapsed on top of me, for goodness' sake! That had nothing to do with the way I had grown up. I told him that God above was my psychiatrist. After all, God was there when I needed him. He had made sure I was found. He had comforted me and given me a new life. The way I saw it, the tragedy I suffered was something I needed to go through in order to know him.

"One of the doctors told me that even after four surgeries I still might not walk again. If I did, it would be with a noticeable limp. I nodded as though I had accepted the news, but silently I was praying, telling God I knew I would walk again someday, but that it would be according to his timetable. And before long I was walking, wearing a brace that extended from my foot to my knee. Once again, I was told I would need the brace for the rest of my life. But it only worked with sneakers, and I'm not a sneakers type of person. I love shoes—all kinds of shoes—and dressing up and being tall. And I love my boots!

"Every day I went to therapy, and I kept wearing my brace, but my faith in Christ was growing so much that I knew that before long I wouldn't need it anymore. By February of 2002 I took the brace off for one minute. I could walk in my bare feet! It wasn't easy but I could do it. I started to laugh out loud because I knew the Lord was strengthening my foot. Then I realized that my boots made the perfect brace, with the leather coming up tight around my calf. Since then, I've made so much progress that I can now wear normal shoes and most people don't even notice that I have a slight limp.

"Sometimes I wonder about Paul, the man who held my hand and calmed me when I thought I couldn't go on. After I got out of the hospital, a reporter interviewed me along with some of the men who rescued me. When I asked about Paul, they seemed puzzled. 'There's no one named Paul on our team,' one of them assured me. But I pressed them: 'Someone was holding my hand for at least twenty minutes when you were digging me out. He told me his name was Paul. I kept reminding myself of his name because I wanted to thank him.'

" 'I'm sorry, but nobody was holding your hand when we were removing the rubble.' Though my story has been told on *Oprah* and *CNN* on television and in *Guideposts* and *Time* magazines, no one named Paul has ever stepped forward to take credit for rescuing me that day. But I know that 'Paul' was God's answer to my prayer for a miracle, a messenger of his love in the midst of my pain.

"Though September 11 was a terrible tragedy, I don't feel any hatred for the people who did this. I know that it's God's job, not mine, to deal with them. And I don't regret the pain and suffering I've experienced, not for one day, because what happened to me was my wake-up call.

"When I told Roger that day in the hospital that we could no longer live together, he insisted we get married and that we try to live the right way. In October I started attending a Bible study at the Brooklyn Tabernacle. On November 7, Roger and I were married and I was baptized at the church. Now we are both wanting to follow the Lord.

"The previous summer we had attended a couple of services at the Brooklyn Tabernacle at the urging of a friend. Though I had really been touched by what I saw and heard, feeling the sermon had been delivered just for me, I hadn't been ready to give up the partying, the carousing. Someday I would do it, I told myself. But not right now. I'm too young, having too much fun.

"But now I tell people, 'Tomorrow is not guaranteed to anyone. You don't know what's going to happen to you. Just like Rosa and I and the old man who was sure the building couldn't collapse—we didn't know what was going to happen to us on September 11. I don't think many people get a second chance like I did. God saved me and he saved me for a reason. He heard my prayer and helped me to survive the worst kind of trouble so that I can live for him today and tell other people about what he's done in my life.' "

Like the cross made of steel girders that was found standing in the midst of the devastation that was Ground Zero—a symbol that has inspired so many people—Genelle Guzman-McMillan, the last survivor of the terrible tragedy of 9/11, stands today as a living reminder of the truth of God's Word. Indeed, *the Lord our God is near to us whenever we pray to him.*

If you have never experienced God in the way that Genelle has, take a moment now to pray the greatest breakthrough prayer you can ever pray. Tell him you want to know Christ personally. Ask him to take hold of your life and forgive your sins. As Genelle reminds us, tomorrow may be too late. Why not pray today so that you can lay hold of God's blessings forever?

CHAPTER FOUR

BREAK-
THROUGH
Promises

*D*id you know that in addition to describing God as Creator, Comforter, and King, the Bible also calls him "the Hearer of Prayer"? This is one of the sweetest yet least known descriptions of the Lord in Scripture: "O you who hear prayer, to you all men will come." Or, more literally, "Hearer of Prayer, to you all men will come" (Psalm 65:2).

If God didn't hear our cries and prayers, wouldn't our world be incredibly lonely and depressing? Fortunately, the Lord is not some distant Creator who set the world in motion and then proceeded to ignore it. He is the "Hearer of Prayer" who made costly provision so that his people might "approach the throne of grace with confidence" (Hebrews 4:16).

BREAKTHROUGH *Prayer*

THE WAY GOD DOES THINGS

God loves to answer our prayers, but the Bible speaks of definite principles that govern a successful approach to him. Just as God created an ordered universe with physical laws governing it, so it is with prayer. Prayer is not some haphazard, accidental undertaking. If we want to experience a real breakthrough, we need to understand and submit to certain spiritual principles.

So what exactly are these principles? To answer that question, consider the way God usually carries out his purposes on earth. What follows is part of a letter written by the prophet Jeremiah from Jerusalem. It was sent to Jewish leaders who were exiles in Babylon along with the greater part of the Hebrew nation. In the letter Jeremiah tells them what the Lord is about to do for his people:

> This is what the LORD says: "When seventy years are completed for Babylon, I will come to you and fulfill my gracious promise to bring you back to this place. For I know the plans I have for you," declares the LORD, "plans to prosper you and not to harm you, plans to give you hope and a future. *Then* you will call upon me and come and pray to me, and I will listen to you. You will seek me and find me when you seek me with all your heart. *I will be found by you*," declares the LORD, "*and will bring you back* from captivity. I will gather you from all the nations and places where I have banished you," declares the LORD, "and will bring you back to the place from which I carried you into exile" (Jeremiah 29:10–14).

Let's analyze the sequence of God's dealings with his people as found in this passage:

1. The Lord has future *plans* for his people that are shaped by his loving-kindness toward them. He never intends them harm, but a future full of his blessings.

2. As a result of his loving purpose, God confirms the *promise* he made that after a period of seventy years, he will bring his people home from exile in Babylon. God's plan for their future comes in the form of a promise that calls for faith on their part.

3. In a part of the sequence that is often overlooked, the Lord says, *"Then* you will call upon me and come and pray to me, and *I will listen to you."*

Will the people seek God and be answered by him *before* or *after* he fulfills his promise to bring them back from captivity? When we read the text carefully, we see that the Israelites were to pray *before* the promised return from exile. The Lord would keep his word to them *after* they fervently prayed for his promise to be fulfilled.

Many of us fail to call on God because we don't understand the need to pray about something God has already promised to do. Though we acknowledge that God has plans for us and that his promises reflect his grace and mercy, we don't realize that he wants us to petition him for the very things he has promised! It's in response to our prayers that God accomplishes his purpose, demonstrating once again that he is a "Hearer of Prayer."

The great reformer Martin Luther boldly declared that God does *nothing* but in answer to prayer. That is probably very close to the truth that Scripture affirms. Over and again, as God deals with his people, we see the same cycle:

Purpose
Promise
Prayer

When the psalmist asserts that the Lord's deliverance is at hand because "the appointed time has come," he quickly adds that God "will respond to the prayer of the destitute; he will not despise their plea" (Psalm 102:13, 17).

Daniel was one of the Israelites living in exile in Babylon. When he heard Jeremiah's prophetic word, promising their eventual return to Jerusalem, he didn't contact his travel agent to secure good seats on the returning caravan. Instead, he "turned to the Lord God and pleaded with him in prayer and petition, in fasting, and in sackcloth and ashes" (Daniel 9:3).

> Many of us fail to call on God because we don't understand the need to pray about something God has already promised to do.

Fasting, sackcloth, and ashes! Why go to such extreme measures when it's all a done deal? Didn't God already give his word to bring the people home from exile? Did Daniel think he could shorten the years of his captivity by fervent prayer? Daniel was neither complacent nor mistaken about what God had said. Rather, he was a godly man who understood that the Lord accomplishes his purposes *in cooperation and partnership* with his people.

Charles Finney, a revivalist of the nineteenth century, maintained that a sure sign of approaching spiritual renewal is that people begin to pray fervently for God to pour out fresh fire as he has promised. Can it be any other way? Where in church history has the promise of spiritual blessing ever been granted except in answer to the prayer of faith?

In the Old Testament, Joel had prophesied that the Holy Spirit would be given to men and women, old and young alike. This was the sure word of God, which Jesus personalized for his disciples just before his ascension to heaven when he said, "You will receive power when the Holy Spirit comes on you; and you will be my witnesses in Jerusalem, and in all Judea and Samaria, and to the ends of the earth" (Acts 1:8). After Jesus ascended, his disciples "joined together constantly in prayer" as they waited for the fulfillment of his promise (Acts 1:14). Purpose, promise, and prayer were joined together once again. To sit idly by because a divine promise had been given would have constituted a misunderstanding of God's intentions.

This is precisely the kind of misunderstanding reflected in modern theology, which places little or no emphasis on prayer. Sadly, many churches live miles below their God-ordained potential because they waste time investigating every church-growth method except the one outlined in the Bible. As Jesus reminded the money changers and merchants in the temple, God wants his house to be called "a house of prayer for all nations" (Mark 11:17). Jesus wasn't laying a legalistic burden on them, but rather pointing out the secret to possessing God's promises. We need to realize that the promises that overflow our Bibles will overflow into our own lives only as we appropriate them through prayer.

But doesn't this gracious plan involving our cooperation with God detract from his glory? It doesn't for three important reasons: God made the plan; God made the promise; and only God can answer prayer! In fact, failing to ask for the resources God has promised indirectly diminishes the praise and honor due his name. Furthermore, we forfeit one of the choice privileges given to the Father's children—the blessing of prayer.

> The promises that overflow our Bibles will overflow into our own lives only as we appropriate them through prayer.

AN OVERLOOKED PROMISE

In the apostle John's first letter we find what I call the most overlooked promise in the Bible. John is speaking about the attitude of assurance God desires for his children.

> I write these things to you who believe in the name of the Son of God so that you may know that you have eternal life (1 John 5:13).

God wants us to feel secure regarding our relationship with him. He wants us to know with certainty that we possess eternal life as part of his family. This security and knowledge is significant because doubts and insecurity will grieve the Father's heart and hinder our ability to live victoriously.

Because we are God's children, then, we can bring our needs to him *with certainty* in prayer. We can have the same confidence in asking for things as we have about our salvation.

Prayer is not some kind of heavenly lottery. Nor does the Bible counsel us to pray with an "I hope this will work" kind of attitude. Instead, we are told that prayer brings us before the throne of grace as children seeking the help of their heavenly Father. That's the heart of breakthrough, successful prayer—the bold confidence that we are talking to the Father who delights to supply our needs. As George Mueller, a nineteenth-century saint, pointed out, "Prayer is not overcoming God's reluctance. It is laying hold of God's willingness."

GUIDELINES TO APPROACHING GOD

Once again, this confident asking and receiving from the Lord must follow the laws of prayer laid down by the Father. These guidelines are found scattered throughout the pages of Scripture. Obedience to them opens up the channel from the Father's willing hand to our own hands stretched out in need.

First, approach God in and through Jesus' name. We make our appeal on the basis of what Christ did for us rather than on our own merits, because we have none. It may be humbling to continually admit that we are helpless sinners saved by grace, but only this path will lead to a prayer-hearing God.

Second, a person who prays must also believe. The Bible states that when we ask, we "must believe and not doubt" or else we will be "double-minded." A doubting, double-minded person "should not think he will receive anything from the Lord" (James 1:6–8). A United States senator once told me that he encourages others to pray even if they don't believe in God because "Hey, you never know!" This philosophy might be effective for betting at a racetrack, but it will not obtain answers from heaven.

The third guideline involves the state of our hearts. The apostle John addresses the issue this way:

> If our hearts do not condemn us, we have *confidence* before God and receive from him *anything* we ask because we obey his commands and do what pleases him (1 John 3:21–22).

A clear conscience and a pure heart are absolute necessities for prevailing prayer. I cannot confidently ask God for answers when I cling to the sins that nailed his Son to the cross of Calvary. I cannot live in iniquity and enjoy the Lord's favor simultaneously. These are impossibilities in God's moral universe. This truth highlights the enormous fallacy of teaching that certain prayers bring success and blessing apart from the spiritual condition of the petitioner. Prayers taken from Scripture, even the Lord's Prayer, will be null and void if people harbor hidden sin in their hearts. "If I regard wickedness in my heart, the Lord will not hear" (Psalm 66:18 NASB).

It may be humbling to continually admit that we are helpless sinners saved by grace, but only this path will lead to a prayer-hearing God.

One Sunday morning, as people gathered to pray at the front of the church after the service, I saw a man motioning me to come and pray for him. When I asked how I could help, he replied that he was requesting prayer for physical healing. But something about him troubled me. When I asked if he was a Christian, he said, "Yeah, of course, I've been in church almost all of my life."

"What church are you presently a member of?" I countered.

"Oh, I kind of just move around as the Spirit leads. I haven't been a member anywhere for years."

For some reason I felt no peace about praying for him. Then I noticed a woman standing a few feet behind him. When I asked about her, he said, "Yeah, that's my girl-friend."

I felt God leading me to ask another question, one that required some boldness.

"Where does she live?" I asked.

"What do you mean, where does she live? I came up for prayer for this problem, and you're asking about my girl-friend?"

I didn't budge, feeling sure God was helping me.

"You know exactly what I mean. Where does she live?"

"Okay, we live together. But God knows I really love her, and we're definitely gonna make it right one day. We have a special relationship that the Lord understands. But forget that—are you gonna pray for my healing or not?"

"Let me get this straight," I answered. "You know the Bible and claim to be a Christian. You're living in fornica-tion with this lady and know that it's wrong before God. And you now want me to ask that same God to heal you *while* you live in this mess. Sir, there's not one chance in a billion that God will answer you or anyone else who prays about it. He would have to violate his Word to hear you.

And if he answered you, he would be encouraging your horrible lifestyle."

I'm not sure he heard the last sentence because he walked out in a huff before I finished speaking. I regretted that, but it was better than carrying on a meaningless charade and failing to tell him the truth as it is in Jesus.

No wonder so many prayers never make it past the ceiling! If we want our petitions to be heard and answered, we cannot violate God's spiritual laws. This is the most difficult part about prayer by far. It's easy to ask God for the things we want and need. But it's not so simple to adjust our hearts and lives to his Word.

Because Satan understands the potential of prayer far better than we, he has developed cunning strategies to clog the asking-receiving channel. An unforgiving spirit, bitterness, secret sexual sins—the list is endless—can stymie our praying. Every sin we hide and justify becomes a hindrance to bold, confident prayer to the Father.

A fourth guideline for effective prayer, one we have already touched upon, is to approach God with assurance. This is the attitude he desires from every believer every time we pray. John says:

> This is the confidence we have in approaching God: that if we ask anything according to his will, he hears us. And if we know that he hears us—whatever we ask—we know that we have what we asked of him (1 John 5:14–15).

John uses an interesting Greek word for "confidence." *Parresia* derives from a root that denotes "all outspokenness," "frankness," or "boldness." It is the confidence of a child so sure of his father's love that he freely speaks all that is in his heart. With God, there is to be no holding back or fear of rejection. It is the same thought we find in Paul's word to the Ephesians: "In him [Christ] and through faith in him we may approach God with freedom and confidence" (Ephesians 3:12).

Yet many of us lack this confidence, and our insecurity about our relationship with God is stifling our prayer life. Instead of bringing our needs confidently to him, we cloak our doubt and unbelief in mock humility. If we really believed God's guarantee to both hear and answer our prayers, we would pray far more than we do. Note the breathtaking import of this overlooked promise. The Lord wants us to be absolutely sure that "if we ask *anything* according to his will, he hears us." If he hears us, "*whatever* we ask, we know that *we have* what we asked of him." What an incredible promise filled with grace and power! Not until we go to heaven will we learn of the mighty things accomplished by this sort of prayer.

> If we really believed God's guarantee to both hear and answer our prayers, we would pray far more than we do.

Because God cannot fail to keep his word, he must, then, answer every petition he hears. But surely God is omnipresent, hearing every sound and voice in the universe. So what exactly does this passage mean by "hears"? It means that certain prayers are "heard" in the receptive, approved sense of being heard, and those requests bring us a present-tense assurance, enabling us to say, "It's mine!"

HOW CAN I KNOW GOD'S WILL?

As always, we must keep in mind that prayer is heard and answered only according to the "house rules." It's not a matter of feeling something, but of being in line with God's way of doing things, with his way of accomplishing his purposes. We can never "use" God when we pray because that would make him the servant in the relationship and put us in charge of the universe. John lays down one vital condition for those who want to pray with this kind of confidence and power: We must ask according to God's will.

What is the prayer God always hears? What is the "anything" he will do for us? When will we have confidence and all-outspokenness in his presence? When can we have present assurance of God's answer? Every time we ask according to his will! Then and only then can the phenomenal potential of this promise become reality. First we must understand and submit to God's will, and then we will have the confidence that he hears us. The Lord has assured us that *every* prayer he hears will be granted, no matter how impossible it seems.

The obvious and critical question is, how can I know I'm asking according to God's will? Carefully studying the Bible reveals the Lord's will and purpose for us. As we rightly "divide" it and meditate upon its promises, the Holy Spirit works in tandem, producing insight and faith and showing us how we should pray. A Christian cannot be powerful in prayer while not living in God's Word.

Still, life is complicated and the application of God's promises is not easy. For this reason, Scripture gives a second guideline:

In the same way, the Spirit helps us in our weakness. We do not know what we ought to pray for, but the Spirit himself intercedes for us with groans that words cannot express (Romans 8:26).

If we let him, the Holy Spirit will be our personal prayer partner. The complexities and heartaches of life can overwhelm us to the point that we can't find words in prayer. Even the apostle Paul experienced this dilemma; he talks about "our weakness" and acknowledges that

> Though intelligible words are not always employed, the Spirit assists us in meeting the conditions of asking according to God's will—the secret of all successful prayer.

"we do not know what we ought to pray for." But the Spirit of God dwells in us to help us pray beyond our limited ability, for "the Spirit intercedes for the saints *in accordance with God's will*" (Romans 8:27). Though intelligible words are not always employed, the Spirit assists us in meeting the conditions of asking according to God's will—the secret of all successful prayer. We need to believe this and be open to the present-day ministry of the Holy Spirit.

I knew a man who struggled mightily with a drinking problem. He was living as a drunk on the streets when he began visiting our services. Though he heard the Word of God, experienced the love of believers, and sought deliverance, he still couldn't stop drinking. He went up and down, month after month, like a yo-yo. Sober one week, drunk the next. We prayed with him, repeatedly explaining the good news of Jesus Christ, but nothing seemed to help.

After dropping out of sight for a while, the man suddenly reappeared toward the end of a Sunday service. I had just finished preaching, and people were praying at the altar. When I opened my eyes, there he stood, looking as though a truck had just run over him. He was filthy and disheveled, with gauze bandages wrapped around one arm like a mummy. He looked up at me with slightly glazed eyes and a hopelessness that broke my heart. Motioning for him to join me on the platform where I was sitting, I asked him what had happened. He told me he'd been in a drunken brawl, and I reminded him that he would likely die in the street if he continued living the way he was. He agreed and, as if to prove it, lifted up one pant leg, revealing a leg that had blown up like a balloon, almost twice the size of the other one.

I didn't know what to say. He had already heard every piece of advice I had to give. The church had tried to help him without success. What more could anyone do? I sat next to him in total silence, not knowing how to pray because there seemed no adequate words. Instead, I quietly asked God for help in ministering to this man. Gradually a deep compassion filled my heart, and I began to weep. I took his bruised hand in mine. I never said one word, but I was praying through the sobs and tears the Spirit gave me. Before long, he was weeping too.

We sat there for a long time, two grown men crying their eyes out without saying a word. While we wept, the Lord was helping both of us as he promised. That night became the turning point for my friend. Soon he was worshiping God every Sunday and learning more about Jesus. He became an usher at our church about a year later. I'll never forget the first time I saw him come forward to assist with the offering. You could hardly tell it was the same man. Smiling as he walked up the aisle, basket in hand, he wore a dark suit with a nice tie. He looked like a regular deacon!

WHAT ABOUT GOD'S SOVEREIGNTY?

Despite the fact that the Bible is clear about our need to pray according to God's will, some churches and Christian teachers place so much importance on God's sovereignty that they fail to emphasize prayer at all. Why make great claims for the power of prayer when God has already predetermined each second of every day? Nothing, including prayer, can change our life situations. To that error, the Bible declares, "You do not have, because you do not ask God" (James 4:2). James did not say the believers lacked because it was God's will that they did. Their failure to ask is what hindered the Almighty from granting what he would have happily given.

This false concept of God's sovereignty is destroying the spiritual potential of churches everywhere. While endless lectures are given about the nature and character of God, prayer meetings are nonexistent. Of course it's important to hear sound Bible teaching, but the real truth about God should lead people to a life of asking and receiving.

WILL GOD GIVE US EVERYTHING WE WANT?

When it comes to understanding the Bible, Satan tries to confuse us by getting us to take positions at extreme ends of the spectrum. For each person who fails to pray because of mistaken notions about God's sovereignty, there is another who prays a great deal but from the wrong motives, as though they, and not God, were in control. So James adds this caution: "When you ask, you do not receive, *because you ask with wrong motives,* that you may spend what you get on your pleasures" (James 4:3).

As my friend Warren Wiersbe says, "God supplies your needs, not your greeds." The idea that we can command God through some "word of faith" to act contrary to his will is ridiculous. This false "faith teaching" has planted foolishness in the pulpits and carnality in the pews. People are "claiming" things that were never promised to New Testament believers while ignoring the spiritual power and grace the world desperately needs. The first rule of prayer is not "faith," but whether the request is according to God's will. Let's not forget that the Lord still sits on his throne as ruler of the universe.

> The first rule of prayer is not "faith," but whether the request is according to God's will.

Even though it can at times be difficult to discern God's will, he will teach us how to pray as we humbly wait for guidance. No matter how confusing a situation may be, we can count on two clear and powerful promises that leave no question about God's will. These two promises can give our prayer life a fresh start so that we can begin praying regularly with confidence:

If any of you lacks wisdom, he should ask God, who gives generously to all without finding fault, and it will be given to him (James 1:5).

My *God will meet all your needs* according to his glorious riches in Christ Jesus (Philippians 4:19).

We can confidently pray, then, for daily wisdom and for our Father to supply every need. Don't permit the size of any problem to prevent you from approaching the throne of grace. Instead, may God's promises propel your prayer so that you are no longer afraid to ask and receive great things from him. "Hearer of Prayer, to you all men will come!"

CHAPTER FIVE

WHEN THE MOUNTAIN *Won't Move*

*S*ometimes life gets so tough that even the most faith-filled Christian has difficulty summoning the faith to pray for a breakthrough. It doesn't matter how many Bible verses you have memorized or how much God has blessed you in the past. A difficult problem or a heart-breaking set of circumstances suddenly mushrooms into a huge, immovable mountain, whose shadow makes it hard for you to envision how God will answer your prayer.

All of us, from the strongest to the weakest, experience such times. But rather than allowing our mountains, however massive, to become obstacles to prayer, we can turn them into opportunities to learn valuable lessons about our level of spiritual maturity and our need to go deeper with God in prayer.

TWO CHALLENGES

Such times of trial and difficulty remind us of two great challenges regarding the prayer of faith. The first challenge is to believe that no situation, however evil or entrenched, is beyond the scope of prayer. In theory we know that God can do anything, but many of us fail to trust him when it comes time to pray for specific people or situations. Instead of looking to the Lord for help, we keep our eyes on the problem, which grows bigger the longer we gaze at it. We don't pray seriously about such problems because they just seem too big, too hard, or too complex for prayer to resolve.

Though we may mentally affirm the promises of Scripture, we fail to lean on them. Reluctant to come before the throne of grace to receive the help God promises, we worry, complain, live in fear and depression, ask others for advice—anything and everything but go to the Lord in prayer. Even we preachers are guilty of this, though we preach every Sunday about an omnipotent God!

The second hurdle is the waiting. Most of us hate to be kept waiting for an answer to prayer. We've asked the Lord to intervene, and we want immediate results. *What's taking him so long?* We feel as though we're holding on for dear life, but the situation hasn't changed one iota. In fact, it's gotten worse! *How long do we have to wait? Is God even interested in us? Does he care about our problems?*

Without learning the secret of how to wait in faith, many of us become spiritually fatigued as we pray. We may start doubting whether God's promises apply to our particular situation. Instead of entertaining this as a reasonable doubt, we need to realize that we are encountering an area of spiritual warfare not often discussed.

I have discovered that the most difficult subjects to write about have to do with the truths people think they already know while their actions prove otherwise. Total ignorance is not what holds us back from growing in God. Instead, we don't grow because we haven't yet fully embraced these all-too-familiar truths. That's what causes us repeated failure, particularly in regard to prayer. Sound doctrine that yields faithless living and no prayer is no doctrine at all. Find a church that doesn't pray and you'll discover a preacher who's not getting to the heart of things no matter how eloquently he preaches. What we really believe is always revealed in the way we talk to God in prayer.

TO WHOM ARE WE PRAYING?

This battle to ask the Lord for great things in prayer and then wait expectantly for the answer has been going on for centuries. Because God understands how hard it is for us to realize that no situation is too big for him, he has filled the sacred Scriptures with reminders of his awesome power. We need these reminders as encouragement whenever we face those big, immovable mountains that challenge our faith.

> Who has measured the waters in the hollow of his hand,
>   or with the breadth of his hand marked off the heavens?
> Who has held the dust of the earth in a basket,
>   or weighed the mountains on the scales
>   and the hills in a balance? . . .

> Surely the nations are like a drop in a bucket;
>> they are regarded as dust on the scales;
>> he weighs the islands as though they were fine dust.
> Lebanon is not sufficient for altar fires,
>> nor its animals enough for burnt offerings.
> Before him all the nations are as nothing;
>> they are regarded by him as worthless
>> and less than nothing (Isaiah 40:12, 15–17).

Although written in figurative language, this passage describes a God so awesome that he considers entire oceans and even the whole universe a small thing! To him mountain ranges are like specks of dirt and the nations themselves are only a drop in the bucket. But there is more:

> He sits enthroned above the circle of the earth,
>> and its people are like grasshoppers.
> He stretches out the heavens like a canopy,
>> and spreads them out like a tent to live in.
> He brings princes to naught
>> and reduces the rulers of this world to nothing.
> No sooner are they planted,
>> no sooner are they sown,
>> no sooner do they take root in the ground,
> than he blows on them and they wither,
>> and a whirlwind sweeps them away like chaff
>> (Isaiah 40:22–24).

Now we see God seated so high above the earth that its inhabitants are like tiny insects running to and fro before him. Presidents, prime ministers, and kings—all those in authority rule only at *his* bidding. Their vaunted armies and impressive missile defense systems are like children's toys before God. With one word from his mouth, he deposes the powerful and sets others in their place.

Isaiah is not exaggerating. This is the great God we worship and serve! Amazingly, he is the One who invites us to call on him in the day of trouble so he can exert his incredible power on our behalf. Best of all, this arrangement was God's idea, not ours. He yearns to intervene in our "impossible" dilemmas, problems that are like child's play for

> God yearns to intervene in our "impossible" dilemmas, problems that are like child's play for him.

him. Knowing our struggle to comprehend the extent of his power, God offers another vivid illustration for us to ponder:

> "To whom will you compare me?
>   Or who is my equal?" says the Holy One.
> Lift your eyes and look to the heavens:
>   Who created all these?
> He who brings out the starry host one by one,
>   and calls them each by name.
> Because of his great power and mighty strength,
>   not one of them is missing (Isaiah 40:25–26).

I remember struggling with a seemingly insurmountable problem one day when I was a young pastor. My difficulty was put into perspective the moment I read a newspaper article about a newly discovered star. This star is so huge that, had it been close to earth, it would not have fit into the space between the earth and the sun! We are talking about a star beyond our wildest imagination, because the sun is 93 million miles away from earth. It occurred to me that this star, magnificent as it is, is merely one of a vast number God created out of nothing and called by name. I dropped my head onto the desk that day and wept for joy at the greatness of God, reassured that my "insurmountable problem" was as nothing to the Lord.

The next time you are faced with an insurmountable problem, I'd advise you to look into the heavens on a clear night. The evidence of God's greatness is right above your head. Scientists say there are about 7,000 stars visible to the naked eye, though only about 2,000 of these can be seen at any one time and place. So even on the clearest night you see less than a third of all the stars visible to people around the world. But that's not the end of it. Recent studies indicate that there are far more stars than the eye can see, perhaps 200 billion—that's 200,000,000,000—in our own galaxy, and the Milky Way is just one of millions of galaxies! Though no one knows exactly how many stars there are, one estimate puts the number at three thousand million billion stars—a three with sixteen zeroes behind it.

As God assures us, the "heavens are the work of [his] hands" (Psalm 102:25). He merely "commanded and they were created" (Psalm 148:5). Just one word from him, and three thousand million billion stars came into being.

What's more, Scripture tells us that God "determines the number of the stars and *calls them each by name*" (Psalm 147:4). Think about it! What "big" problem are you facing right now that is too hard for him? What possible need is beyond his ability to supply?

Do you remember when God promised to make Abraham the father of many children even though he was an old man married to Sarah, who was herself old and barren? The Lord promised Abraham that his offspring would be so numerous that they couldn't be counted, saying, "I will make your offspring like the dust of the earth, so that if anyone could count the dust, then your offspring could be counted" (Genesis 13:16). On a later occasion, the Lord told Abraham to "look up at the heavens and count the stars—if indeed you can count them. . . . So shall your offspring be" (Genesis 15:5).

I wonder if that second comparison seemed like a bit of a comedown to Abraham. Even though he could see a sky full of stars—as many as 2,000—surely the grains of dust on the earth were of a far greater number. But God had in mind things Abraham couldn't possibly see. Science has shown us that the number of stars in all the galaxies could be as great as the dust of the earth. What a tribute to the accuracy of the Bible and the greatness of God. Look up at night into the heavens and let every star inspire you to do what Abraham did that evening—he believed the Lord.

> God "determines the number of the stars and calls them each by name." What "big" problem are you facing right now that is too hard for him?

WHEN YOU WANT TO GIVE UP

I have seen God do many wonderful things over the course of my life, yet I still encounter times when my faith is severely challenged. Not long ago, I met a young woman who badly needed God's help. At first it seemed as though the church might be able to do something. Then, just as we were making progress, we were suddenly faced with an insurmountable problem—a mountain we couldn't climb over, couldn't sidestep, and couldn't budge. Her difficulties seemed so complex, so entrenched. The solution seemed impossible to find. Maybe I had to let this one go, I thought. I was out of ideas and nearly out of faith.

Farah was born in Haiti, the poorest country in the Western hemisphere. But it wasn't the stifling poverty that hurt her as much as the sense of abandonment she felt when her mother left for America shortly after she was born. She ended up living with her father and a stepmother in the rooming house they owned.

From the time she was six, Farah was sexually abused by her stepmother's brother and various male boarders. Convinced no one would believe her if she spoke up, she kept the nightmare secret. Then one day her father went off to work and never returned home. Quickly she was shunted off to an aunt, who died soon after from AIDS. Then she went to her grandmother's home.

Finally, at the age of ten, Farah came to the United States to live with her mother. Full of dreams of America and a happier life, she hoped her parents might even get back together. But by then, Farah's mother had a young child and was living with another man. That child, not Farah, became the apple of her eye, and Farah's life turned into a long episode of weeping and bitter tears. She was a shattered, frightened little girl whom nobody seemed to love.

If this were a movie, the good guy would have rushed into her story right about now, just in time to make the rescue. That's what Farah thought when a school security guard began taking an interest in her life. He started by walking her home on a regular basis. Before long, she gave him her phone number. But her knight in shining armor turned out to be a thirty-six-year-old sexual predator, intent on initiating a relationship with a twelve-year-old girl. Convinced she had found true love, young Farah was determined to cling to the only "solid" relationship she had. Her rebelliousness and inner anger surfaced when her mother objected to the relationship.

Deciding she couldn't cope with the situation, her mother shipped Farah off to Florida, where her father was then living with yet another wife. While there, Farah decided to open her wounded heart, telling him about the abuse she had suffered in the past. Incredibly, instead of sympathy, it triggered more sexual abuse, this time from her own father.

By then, Farah hardly had the will to live. Still, she was a bright girl who managed to do well in school despite her emotional turmoil. Eventually her stepmother became suspicious of the relationship between Farah and her father and shipped her back to New York. It wasn't long until Farah began living with the security guard in his apartment in Brooklyn.

After a while, a friend began inviting her to visit the Brooklyn Tabernacle. But Farah was not interested in religion. She had dabbled with Jehovah's Witness and Mormon teachings and concluded they held no answers. Yet her friend persisted, and Farah finally relented, agreeing to attend a service. For the first time in her life, she heard the best news possible: There is a God in heaven, and he loves her. She felt something powerful, yet tender, wooing her toward the light. Farah wanted to open her heart to Jesus, but a dark stronghold held her back from full surrender. The battle for her soul raged on.

For the first time in her life, Farah heard the best news possible: There is a God in heaven, and he loves her.

Farah had become pregnant, and the pregnancy ended in a miscarriage. It happened when she was alone one day at her high school. That experience sent her into a deeper depression, but one that made her envy the joy-filled Christians who stayed in contact with her. At nineteen, she became pregnant again and gave birth to a daughter. Her mother was so shamed by the news that she turned her back on Farah and her granddaughter.

Farah tried to overcome her attachment to her boyfriend, but by now she had been with him for nearly half her life. Through the years an emotional and physical bond had been forged that seemed impossible to break. One time she even moved back into his apartment after he had kicked her out.

Finally, during another visit to the Brooklyn Tabernacle, Farah cried out, "God, you have to come and help me!" One of the associate pastors learned of Farah's situation and immediately referred her to me. That Tuesday night, when Farah came to my office, I saw only a pretty twenty-one-year-old Haitian girl clutching a child in her arms. I hadn't a clue about her painful past or about her fear of meeting me, convinced as she was that I would throw her out of the church as soon as I heard her story.

Tears filled my eyes as she told me that story. Anger and revulsion rose up in me as I thought about the man who had seduced her. I began by assuring Farah that the most important thing she could do was to begin a new relationship with the Lord, trusting him for the answers she needed. But what exactly was God's plan for Farah's life? She had so little going for her—no self-respect, no supportive family, and a young daughter to care for. *One thing is for sure,* I thought. *Only the Lord can deliver and heal this fractured life.*

But what about the immediate issues? Where would she live? She had no money for an apartment of her own. Her mother wouldn't take her in, and she had nowhere else to go. I wondered whether she would even agree to leave this sick relationship if given the chance.

There in my office I prayed with Farah, reassuring her of God's incredible love and mercy. I reminded her that no situation is too hard for him. In return, she told me she wanted to serve the Lord by putting her trust in him. Encouraged by her response, I promised that the church would stick with her, walking with her every step of the way. She wasn't alone, I said, because Jesus specializes in healing shattered lives.

There were still many unanswered questions, but I was beginning to see some light at the end of the tunnel. Over the next few days I dealt with the security guard and then found a couple in our church who would take Farah in until we could get a handle on the situation. Things definitely seemed to be looking up.

I was trusting God to direct the next step, eager to see what he would do, when Farah walked into my office one day looking downcast. It seems I had been a little late in helping her out of that ugly relationship—she was pregnant again! The news took the wind right out of my sails. It was one thing to provide for Farah and her daughter—something I still hadn't figured out—but now a second baby was on the way. I knew plenty of people who would help a young woman get back on her feet, but it was a totally different thing to find that kind of help for a woman with two small children. That was a much bigger job. Suddenly all my sermons on faith, all my memories of God's faithfulness receded into the shadow cast by the mountain that loomed before me. I sat speechless as Farah wept quietly.

I had no answers for this unhappy young woman. Her already complicated situation had rapidly worsened. Not knowing where in the world to turn to for help, I turned to God in prayer. As I prayed silently in my spirit, the Lord surprised me by sparking a tiny ember of hope. Satan would not have the last word in this whole thing after all! The Lord would somehow make a way in this wilderness of trouble. A holy anger rose within me: "God, help us. Please show us what to do!" As I prayed, my sinking heart of unbelief was replaced by a firm trust in the Almighty God. I told Farah to stop crying because God was going to give us a breakthrough!

Right then I was reminded of a godly couple in New Hampshire who headed up New Life, the finest ministry for troubled young women that I knew of. I asked my secretary to reach them by phone.

"Hello! George, I've got a situation here and wonder if you can help. It's very complicated, but the bottom line is, we're fighting for a young lady's life."

I outlined the facts, including Farah's daughter and the newly discovered pregnancy. I told George she needed to get out of the city and away from the temptation to return to that man. She needed to have her mind renewed so she could develop a fresh outlook on life. I pointed out that she was only twenty-one years old and had her whole life ahead of her. But who could minister to her and care for two children at the same time? I asked. I held my breath as I waited for George's answer.

"Brother, I don't know what to say," George responded.

Please don't say anything if you're going to say no, I thought.

"I don't know what to say except we'll do our best to make room for Farah and her children. God will help us somehow. How soon can you get her up here for an interview?"

That day God was gracious, not only to a broken young woman from Haiti, but also to a pastor whose faith had begun to falter.

Elated, I told Farah the good news, filling her in on all that New Life had to offer. She was relieved to know that someone was willing to take her. Not only that, she and her children would be well cared for, living in the New England mansion that housed New Life's ministry.

What a tender, compassionate God we have! That day he was gracious, not only to a broken young woman from Haiti, but also to a pastor whose faith had begun to falter. No wonder our God is called "Wonderful, Counselor" (Isaiah 9:6 KJV)!

About a year later, I preached in Manchester, New Hampshire, at the church George pastors. Farah was in church that day, and it was the first time I had seen her since she left New York. Before I spoke, she asked if I would dedicate her infant son that evening. She handed me her child as I stood behind the pulpit, and I'll never forget the radiant, joyful look on her face. No one in the congregation could understand the emotion I felt as I held that baby in my arms and lifted my voice to God. As I prayed, Farah stood with her hands held high in worship, thanking the One who had done so much for her. It was all too much for me. I wept aloud and unashamedly.

Because of what the Lord has done in her life, Farah knows there is no limit to God's power. She understands that he is always ready to help those who call out to him in believing prayer. Like a father who pities his children, the Lord always listens to our cries. His power and love, as Farah later told that congregation in New Hampshire, can heal us in places only he can touch.

Through God's forgiveness, Farah has learned to forgive herself and others. Despite a past filled with the worst kind of abuse, she is not bitter in spirit but tender and loving. Like someone who has been raised from the dead, she has been given a future full of hope. The hurting, little girl who craved a sense of "family" is now surrounded by God's love made real through others.

God wants you to know that his answers are always worth waiting for! But remember, while you're waiting, Satan might whisper that you are alone and forsaken. Never forget God's word of assurance: "Can a mother forget the baby at her breast and have no compassion on the child she has borne? *Though she may forget, I will not forget you!*" (Isaiah 49:15). And again, "God has said, *'Never will I leave you; never will I forsake you'*" (Hebrews 13:5).

> Keep holding onto the Lord today no matter how you feel, no matter how bad things get.

Keep holding onto the Lord today no matter how you feel, no matter how bad things get.

People can't always be relied on, sometimes not even family members. But God will never fail us. The Bible says, "Since ancient times no one has heard, no ear has perceived, no eye has seen any God besides you, *who acts on behalf of those who wait for him*" (Isaiah 64:4). The truth of God's faithfulness was so ingrained on King David's heart that he reminded himself of it with these words: "My soul, *wait silently for God alone*, for my expectation is from Him" (Psalm 62:5 NKJV). David was encouraged the same way as Isaiah later on—because the Lord had promised that "they shall not be ashamed who wait for Me" (Isaiah 49:23 NKJV). No man or woman has ever been let down by trusting in God!

If you have been waiting for an answer to prayer for a long time, remember that long waits often occur right before the biggest mountains come down. Keep praying and don't give in to the doubt or fear that tells you "this situation is impossible" or "that person will never change" or "it's just too late." Instead of letting Satan have the last word in the battle to believe, speak it yourself, borrowing from God's own word in Scripture: "*The LORD is faithful to all his promises* and loving toward all he has made" (Psalm 145:13).

CHAPTER SIX

BREAK THROUGH
to Fruitfulness

When I was growing up in Brooklyn, basketball was my thing. I would shovel snow off the playground court a block from my home just so I could practice shooting on cold Saturday mornings. By the time other kids would arrive, I was half-frozen but still ready to shoot hoops. I spent years worrying about whether I would be tall enough to compete effectively. My mom wasn't happy about my preoccupation because I left pencil lines all over the walls of our house, trying to mark how much I had grown from month to month.

SPIRITUAL GROWTH

I wish we Christians today were as concerned about our spiritual growth as I was back then about my physical growth, because the Bible has much to say on this important subject. Of course, it's easy to keep track of physical growth, but how can we tell if we're growing spiritually? Scripture offers the only standard by which we can measure ourselves.

When Jesus declared, "You must be born again" (John 3:7), he was making an analogy between physical birth and spiritual rebirth. Being "born again" involves the act of receiving God's salvation. But just as physical birth is a beginning point for physical growth, being born again is the beginning point for spiritual growth. It is vital to remember that we have the capacity to grow spiritually in much the same way that flowers, trees, and babies grow physically. Scripture tells us we are to "grow in the grace and knowledge of our Lord and Savior Jesus Christ" (2 Peter 3:18). Further, we are exhorted to "crave pure spiritual milk, so that by it you may grow up in your salvation" (1 Peter 2:2).

Sadly, much of the church today has lost this emphasis on spiritual growth and has instead become preoccupied with mere churchgoing and mental affirmations of doctrinal truths. How many Christians can testify to an ongoing growth in God? I fear that many of us have mistaken outward observances for spiritual growth, being unaware of God's plan for the healthy development of our spiritual lives. The prophet Hosea said,

"I will be like the dew to Israel;
    he will *blossom* like a lily.
Like a cedar of Lebanon
    he will *send down his roots;*

his young shoots will grow.
His splendor will be like an olive tree,
    his fragrance like a cedar of Lebanon" (Hosea 14:5–6).

Note the words God uses when talking about his people: "he will *blossom* ... he will send down his *roots* ... young shoots will *grow* ... His splendor will be like an olive *tree* ... like a *cedar* of Lebanon." Hosea is describing not a mechanical process, but an organic one. He is talking not about mere membership in a particular church, but about a spiritual process of continual growth, one that fulfills the scriptural promise that says, "God ... makes things grow" (1 Corinthians 3:7). If we fail to display signs of spiritual growth, either something is terribly wrong with us or we never had life from God to begin with.

How sad it is that when asked about their spiritual life, many have nothing more to say than "I'm a Baptist" or "I'm a Catholic" or "I'm charismatic." How unrelated this all is to God's description of what is truly vital:

The righteous will *flourish* like a palm tree,
    they will grow like a cedar of Lebanon; ...
They will still *bear fruit* in old age,
    they will stay *fresh and green* (Psalm 92:12, 14).

The goal of this growth process is that we are to *bear fruit*. God is not as interested in what we "do" for him as in our bearing spiritual fruit. That's the kind of breakthrough he's looking for. And only his Spirit at work within us can produce the godly character he desires.

A lack of spiritual fruit, therefore, is a serious matter to the Lord. It's the reason that Israel was rejected by God and driven from the Promised Land: "Ephraim [Israel] is blighted, their root is withered, *they yield no fruit*" (Hosea 9:16).

If the Lord is so concerned about fruit bearing, we need to ask why many church leaders today seem preoccupied with attendance figures and the latest church growth techniques. Consider Paul's prayer for the believers in Colossae:

> We pray this in order that you may live a life worthy of the Lord and may please him in every way: *bearing fruit* in every good work, *growing* in the knowledge of God (Colossians 1:10).

Paul entreated the believers to "live a life worthy of the Lord." His words imply that the opposite was also possible: they could live in a manner *unworthy* of their Savior. What did Paul mean by saying they should live a life worthy of Christ? He simply meant that they should *grow* in grace and *bear fruit* to the glory of God. "*This* is to my Father's glory that *you bear much fruit,* showing yourselves to be my disciples" (John 15:8). God is glorified as his Spirit bears fruit in and through us.

Fruitfulness, in fact, is the only evidence that someone is a genuine Christian. The evidence of faith doesn't consist of what you claim with your lips, your membership in a particular church, or the creed you espouse. Walking into a church doesn't make you a Christian anymore than walking into a garage makes you a car! What a frightful shock it will be for countless "decent, religious" folks to discover on Judgment Day the truth about God's salvation.

We know that the law is incapable of saving anyone because the law is a *lifeless* thing written in stone. But

Christ suffered, died, and rose again so that we would die to the law and "belong to another, to him who was raised from the dead, *in order that we might bear fruit* to God" (Romans 7:4). Bearing fruit is vital since it is the underlying purpose behind the gift of God's Son.

Walking into a church doesn't make you a Christian anymore than walking into a garage makes you a car!

A new believer in Christ will *always* exhibit a change in behavior as proof that the fruit-bearing process has begun. Paul told the Colossians, "All over the world *this gospel is bearing fruit and growing* just as it has been doing among you since the day you heard it and understood God's grace in all its truth" (Colossians 1:6). I am concerned about all the false sermons being preached today, sermons that water down the true gospel and its power toward those who really believe. A growing number of churches, afraid of "scaring" people away, have become more intent on being seeker-sensitive than on trusting God to transform lives, as he has been doing for two thousand years. We needn't worry about the power of the gospel, for *it still is* the power of God for salvation. We just need to be bold enough to communicate it in simplicity and love.

Because many churches have drifted away from God's supernatural formula for growth, we now confront the dilemma of countless "converts" and church members who haven't really been converted. What's the proof of this? Lives that don't exhibit the fruit that comes from the Holy

Spirit. If this sounds harsh or judgmental, consider the words of our Lord:

> *"By their fruit* you will recognize them. Do people pick grapes from thornbushes, or figs from thistles? Likewise every good tree bears good fruit, but a bad tree bears bad fruit. A good tree cannot bear bad fruit, and a bad tree cannot bear good fruit. Every tree that does not bear good fruit is cut down and thrown into the fire. Thus, *by their fruit you will recognize them"* (Matthew 7:16–20).

Although Jesus offered this teaching in the context of a warning about false prophets, its application is universal. It doesn't matter how good a preacher you are or whether your ministry seems to have been confirmed by supernatural signs or whether you have memorized most of the Bible. All that is secondary to the question of fruit bearing. The only indisputable proof that God's grace is at work in us is the spiritual fruit we produce. This is neither legalism nor mysticism, but a fact of life in the kingdom of God. As Jesus succinctly put it, "A tree is recognized by its fruit" (Matthew 12:33).

In the mad rush to find the next "cutting-edge ministry" or to experience sensational new "manifestations of the Spirit," many of us have totally forgotten this solemn word of caution from God. It is the proper antidote for superficial theology that is centered on secondary matters.

> "Not everyone who says to me, 'Lord, Lord,' will enter the kingdom of heaven, but only he who does the will of my Father who is in heaven. *Many will say to me* on that day, 'Lord, Lord, did we not prophesy in your name, and in your name drive out demons and perform many mira-

cles?' Then I will tell them plainly, '*I never knew you. Away from me, you evildoers!*'" (Matthew 7:21–23).

Understanding how prophecy, miracles, and delivering people from demons in Christ's name could be met with such ominous words of judgment is not all that important. Rather, we need to remember that a life that bears fruit is the only kind God accepts.

Remember, too, that Israel was rejected by its own Messiah because it did not bear fruit: "Therefore I tell you that the kingdom of God will be taken away from you and given to *a people who will produce its fruit*" (Matthew 21:43).

When God plants a seed and supplies everything needed for the seed to grow, he expects it to bear fruit. If because of its own carelessness it doesn't, he will make changes. The Jewish religious establishment took pride in its doctrinal purity and worship traditions, but these were merely a cover-up for spiritual barrenness. Jesus saw through them and pronounced their doom even though he wept over the city of Jerusalem. Years earlier, John the Baptist had prophesied about this same process: "The ax is already at the root of the trees, and *every tree that does not produce good fruit* will be cut down and thrown into the fire" (Matthew 3:10).

What an awesome word about God's own covenant people! They were descendants of Abraham, possessed the Promised Land, yet were spiritually barren. We who serve God's people today must put more stress on the necessity of spiritual growth in Christ. Only then will obedience to God become habitual through the supernatural flow of his life within us. Let us not forget the terrible alternative from the lips of Jesus: "He [God] cuts off every branch in me that bears no fruit" (John 15:2).

The church today needs a major breakthrough into the kind of fruitful living that pleases the Lord. I fear that too often we are being converted and discipled by the world rather than the other way around. Our influence is negligible. Why is it that two of the largest Christian denominations in the United States have shown zero growth for the last few years despite the nationwide soul-searching after 9/11?

Each month I am flooded by e-mails and letters from people who want to escape a life of spiritual barrenness. People want to see more prayer in their churches, but the deacon board or pastor squelches the idea. The people long to see unbelievers come to Christ, but converts are few and far between. Most of all, these people want to experience the Spirit of God personally in a new and deeper dimension. They hunger to know Jesus better.

THE FRUIT OF GOD'S SPIRIT

What will that new, more fruitful life look like? What is the fruit that pleases and glorifies the Lord? In the truest sense, spiritual fruit never comes from us. It is, instead, a product of the grace of God working in us:

> But the fruit of the Spirit is love, joy, peace, patience, kindness, goodness, faithfulness, gentleness and self-control (Galatians 5:22–23).

Only the Holy Spirit can produce the fruitful living God requires. The Bible says that the Spirit lives inside every true Christian and stands ready to make us a display window for the beauty of Christ. Foremost among all his fruit bearing is *love*. Some Bible commentators believe that love is *the* fruit of the Spirit and the other graces listed are different characteristics of this love.

Without love, every form of religious observance is worthless. Proficiency in Scripture is just a deception. We may understand the divine attributes or probe into the mysteries of predestination, but without love we have no proof of citizenship in heaven. We may perform miracles and preach eloquently, but all our efforts are for nothing if we do not have love. Even the most difficult sacrifices are nothing if they are made without love:

> If I give all I possess to the poor and surrender my body to the flames, but have not love, I gain nothing (1 Corinthians 13:3).

Because God is love, the most prominent character trait of a Christian should be love. Shouldn't congregations that bear the name "Christian" be places of acceptance, mercy, and grace? After all, the apostle John clearly used love as the test to distinguish the true from the counterfeit.

> Dear friends, let us love one another, for love comes from God. Everyone who loves has been born of God and knows God. Whoever does not love *does not know God,* because *God is love* (1 John 4:7–8).

What an incredibly bold statement! People who don't love others cannot know God no matter what religious heritage they claim. It's not whether you read the King James Version or the New International Version that matters. Nor is it about knowledge of Scripture or insights into prophecy. Speaking in tongues or having the gift of healing doesn't define our spiritual condition either. The sign of God's presence is always love.

A life of little love, then, equates with only a scant understanding of God. That can be true of learned theologians as much as of ordinary churchgoers. "Growing in the Lord" will always be characterized by an increase in love. Much of the church today is engrossed in secondary issues. I fear we have "majored on the minors" for so long, we have developed religious cultures that totally contradict the Jesus we claim to preach. The saddest part is, we're so accustomed to this false version of Christianity that we don't want to change it. If this sounds radical or overly negative, read on.

> The saddest part is, we're so accustomed to this false version of Christianity that we don't want to change it.

THE GREATEST DECEPTION

How many churches in America on any given Sunday are eager to have *any and every person* enter their doors? I mean white, black, Latino, gay, homeless, rich or poor, clean or dirty, drugged up or slightly inebriated. Jesus Christ shed his precious blood for *everyone* on earth and never turned away anyone who sincerely came to him for help. We know that the angels of heaven rejoice when *any* unbeliever repents, and we claim that God's love reaches out to the worst prodigal among us. But do our churches reflect the Savior's heart? Do pastors and congregations wait with open arms for the worst of sinners to enter their sanctuaries?

What does it matter how well we know the Bible if we don't aggressively love the folks Christ died for? What good are the gifts of the Spirit if they're only for people like us—people we feel comfortable with? Is this Christianity? Is it found anywhere in the Bible? The greatest deception of all has nothing to do with New Age philosophy or the occult. Rather, it is the idea that we can represent and preach Christ while being strangers to his heart of love.

Sadly, the church growth movement has attempted to legitimize much of our racial prejudice and lack of love for people who are different from us. With no scriptural basis whatsoever, we now have yuppie churches, generation-X churches, and all-white, middle-class congregations that somehow never become integrated even though they are located in cities with high minority populations. Rather than being embarrassed, the so-called experts boldly proclaim that this is the secret to success—but everyone knows what's really going on. And it's not all that new. Many evangelical and Pentecostal denominations were born with strong racist overtones, and love for those who are "other" is still not part of their portfolio.

I have heard just about every justification and cover-up for this sad state of affairs. People have told me that I can't understand "the problem" because I'm not from their part of the country. Preachers have told me they are happy to start another church downtown for the "poor and down-trodden" but they can't risk lots of members leaving if their own doors open up to everyone. Others tell me that "twice a year we join together with minority churches in a big rally." "Seeker-sensitive" technicians have even asserted that it's impossible to have a growing church unless you focus on a homogeneous target group.

How can the world put any stock in Christianity if we practice this kind of exclusivity? Attendance at football games is interracial, people of different races work together in office buildings across the country, and all professional and collegiate athletic programs are now integrated. But as soon as eleven o'clock rolls around on Sunday morning, churches around the country form strange, segregated enclaves that don't reflect life in America.

> The greatest deception of all has nothing to do with New Age philosophy or the occult. Rather, it is the idea that we can represent and preach Christ while being strangers to his heart of love.

Both black and white ministers sometimes cunningly reinforce these prejudices and fears so they can hold the crowd and keep money coming into the church. Although they might keep their own congregations happy, I worry for them in the end. Warning of apostasy in the last days, the book of Jude graphically describes godless men who "have secretly slipped in among you ... autumn trees, *without fruit*" (Jude 4, 12).

Recently a minister-friend asked if I would greet some longtime friends of his while they were in New York. The couple attended one of our Sunday services, and I noticed that both wept during the meeting and also seemed to feel uncomfortable. After the service, I invited them into my office to chat for a while.

During our conversation I asked how their church was doing. The husband said that their pastor of almost forty years was soon retiring and that church membership had been on the decline for some years. Trying to encourage him, I remarked that hopefully God would use the next pastor to lead the church forward.

Both the husband and wife just stared at the floor. I could sense their nervousness as we sat in silence. Then the husband blurted out, in a quavering voice, "Well, you know, we don't allow black people in our church. There's no sign up on the door, mind you, but *they know.*" The man spoke with deep shame and a conviction of sin. I hardly knew what to say to his confession.

I knew that some of the greatest Bible expositors in America had preached in this man's church, going back many decades. I was sure the church's doctrinal statement was orthodox. No doubt it stood valiantly for the divine inspiration of Scripture, and no one had ever accused it of propagating heresy. But what did any of that matter if the church could not love? What kind of sermons were preached in that church if they didn't produce love for souls?

Never forget the following, no matter how pretty someone wants to paint the picture:

1. "A tree is recognized by its fruit."
2. "Whoever does not love does not know God, because God is love."

It grieves me that in the twenty-first century there are still "Christian churches" that won't welcome men and women of another race even though Christ died for them. You can try all day to explain it away, but you can't escape the evil and hypocrisy of it.

No wonder the Spirit of God is a stranger to so many churches across the land. He was sent to tenderly draw people to Christ, yet some congregations are shunning part of the world Christ died for. This sin—and there is no other word for it—is at the top of the list of things holding back spiritual revival. Pornography, immorality, and materialism are ugly sins that have slain their thousands, but who can measure the damage done to the kingdom of God by barren, bigoted churchgoers? How could God send showers of blessing upon unrepentant congregations who practice loveless discrimination?

> The sin—and there is no other word for it—of racial discrimination is at the top of the list of things holding back spiritual revival.

I fear that so-called "fundamentalists" are often the worst culprits when it comes to this kind of hypocrisy. They proudly thump their Bibles and spend time hunting for anything that smacks of heresy. Unfortunately for them, they may one day be revealed as the worst heretics of all.

If anyone says, "I love God," yet hates his brother, he is a liar. For anyone who does not love his brother, whom he has seen, cannot love God, whom he has not seen. And he has given us this command: *Whoever loves God must also love his brother* (1 John 4:20–21).

As I travel around the country, I witness firsthand the spiritual hardness and bigotry that disgraces the name of Christ. I write about it here with deep sadness because God's kingdom suffers reproach on account of the absence of Christlike love among his people. At the judgment seat of Christ we will all have to give an account of our own fruit bearing.

If you recognize yourself or your church in what I have said, find a quiet place to be with God. Humble yourself in his presence and ask him to purge you of all that is unkind and hurtful. May all of us seek his face today for a personal revival that will bear fruit to the praise of the glory of his grace.

CHAPTER SEVEN

A BREAK-THROUGH *Word*

*F*inding new power in prayer always means developing a new relationship with the Word of God, because God's Word provides the right foundation for a life of asking and receiving. Only the prayer of faith secures answers, and we are not left in the dark about how faith is produced:

> Faith comes from *hearing* the message, and the message is heard through *the word* of Christ (Romans 10:17).

How we feel, how things seem, what others say—these transient sentiments and circumstances will never cause faith to take root in our souls. Anyone who relies on them will never be able to pray with confidence before the throne of grace. Instead, we need to develop a strong faith, based on God's unalterable Word. How we react to his Word and the place it finds in our hearts are what will determine our future in God.

The Word is living and powerful, provoking different reactions in different people and even different attitudes within one person. The Word of God that transforms one person may be rejected by another. The truth that lifts us spiritually one day may produce doubts that later tempt us to despair. It is through these intimate dealings with the Word of God that power in prayer is obtained.

Nowhere in the Bible is this better illustrated than in God's "word" to Moses. After fleeing Egypt, Moses lived in isolation from the affairs of men for forty years. Then one day, Israel's future deliverer encountered the Lord in a burning bush (Exodus 3). That day in the desert, Moses listened as the Lord revealed his name. He witnessed miraculous signs confirming that God had spoken and commissioned him. Then God gave Moses a message to deliver to both the Hebrew elders and Pharaoh: "Let my people go." What a message to carry to a people enslaved for generations! What a message to deliver to one of the kings who had enslaved them! Though Moses at first shrank from the mission, he later obeyed and went to Egypt.

WHICH WORD?

Before exploring what happened next, let's clarify what is meant by the "word of the Lord" so we can more easily apply this story to our own lives. The "word of the Lord" has several meanings in the life of the believer. First and foremost, it stands for the truth of Holy Scripture. The

Bible is the only rule of faith and doctrine for Christians. Every utterance from a preacher, teacher, church leader, or angel is to be compared with the truth of Scripture. No matter what anyone says, the Holy Spirit will never contradict the Bible he inspired.

Second, the "word" can refer especially to the message of Christ or the gospel. The New Testament uses it in this manner with emphasis on the power inherent in the good news of Jesus toward those who believe.

Third, a "word" from God through the Holy Spirit helps define the calling on one's life, either as a commissioning for specific service or as a directive enabling someone to fulfill God's purpose. Examples of this abound in the New Testament, such as the story of how Paul and Barnabas started their missionary work:

> While they were worshiping the Lord and fasting, *the Holy Spirit said,* "Set apart for me Barnabas and Saul for the work to which I have called them" (Acts 13:2).

Notice that this was not a word from the Old Testament that could be read. Neither was it part of New Testament doctrine for the edification of the church. This word was a present-tense directive of the Holy Spirit regarding Paul and Barnabas. The church at Antioch received it as God's word and sent the two men off to fulfill it. Although this word from God didn't involve a moral injunction binding on the rest of us, those to whom it applied needed to believe and obey it.

The Spirit is still alive and active on the earth. No passage in the Bible teaches us to no longer expect the Holy

Spirit's word of guidance in whatever manner he might bring it. The Spirit still desires to guide, but he needs people with an ear to hear what he's saying.

> The Spirit still desires to guide, but he needs people with an ear to hear what he's saying.

Fourth, the "word" of promise from the Bible is applied by the Spirit to our personal situations. Throughout history, godly men and women have faced situations in which the will of God was not plainly evident. Uncertain about what to do or how to pray, they searched Scripture, and the Lord led them to a verse or passage that they believed had a direct bearing on the problem at hand. The autobiographies of great saints are replete with incidences of this kind of encouragement and direction.

RECEIVING THE WORD

When Moses arrived in Egypt, he knew exactly what God wanted him to say. He began by sharing his message with the Hebrew leaders:

> Moses and Aaron brought together all the elders of the Israelites, and Aaron told them everything the LORD had said to Moses.... And when they heard that the LORD was concerned about them and had seen their misery, they bowed down and worshiped (Exodus 4:29–31).

God was about to do something great and announced it beforehand to his chosen people. They received it with praise, much to Moses' delight. Perhaps his mission would prove easier than he had thought. But Moses had yet to deliver God's word to the man least likely to listen.

> Afterward Moses and Aaron went to Pharaoh and said, "This is what the LORD, the God of Israel, says: 'Let my people go, so that they may hold a festival to me in the desert.'" Pharaoh said, "Who is the LORD, that I should obey him and let Israel go? I do not know the LORD and I will not let Israel go" (Exodus 5:1–2).

The same word that was joyfully received by an enslaved people met with mocking disdain from Pharaoh. So don't be surprised when you encounter this kind of ridicule, a common response to God's word. After all, God is at work, separating out a remnant of people as his own through the preaching of the gospel, though the "pharaohs" have always been in the majority.

Remember, too, that the teaching and miracles of Jesus himself failed to convert most of Jerusalem. Our task is not to widen the narrow road as if God needs help to build his church. Instead, we need to be faithful in delivering the message. God will take care of the results. Keep in mind how the apostle Paul described his own ministry:

> For we are to God the aroma of Christ among those who are being saved and those who are perishing. To the one we are the smell of death; to the other, the fragrance of life (2 Corinthians 2:15–16).

Any ministry that is faithful to God will reap a harvest, but it will also confront the mocking rejection of multitudes. Unfortunately, the wide road still has lots of folks on it.

Pharaoh's adamant refusal must have tested Moses' faith in the success of his mission.

> But the king of Egypt said, "Moses and Aaron, why are you taking the people away from their labor? Get back to your work!" Then Pharaoh said, "Look, the people of the land are now numerous, and you are stopping them from working" (Exodus 5:4–5).

Moses must have been startled by the hostility that the word of the Lord produced against him. Where was the fulfillment he was anticipating? Where was God? He had mustered the courage to deliver God's message only to be falsely accused of leading a wildcat labor strike against the nation!

When D. L. Moody began his evangelistic work in Chicago, he wasn't applauded, but instead nicknamed "Crazy Moody" because of his zeal and unorthodox methods. (He had the bizarre notion that God loved poor, dirty street urchins and wanted them saved. Church leaders rejected this "radical" departure from the status quo and secretly sneered at his lack of seminary training.) Nevertheless, D. L. Moody trusted the marching orders the Lord gave him. He became the greatest evangelist of his time but, like Moses, had to face misunderstanding and ridicule.

Yet Pharaoh wasn't content to merely say no to God. He gave orders that the slaves would no longer be given straw for making bricks even though they would be required to meet the same quotas. Instead of producing deliverance, the word of the Lord had produced a worse predicament for everyone. The God who had promised to be with Moses when he appeared to him in the desert seemed not to have made the trip to Egypt.

JIM CYMBALA

THE WORD WILL TEST US

This is the test for anyone who clings to "thus says the Lord." After we pray or step out in obedience, things may get worse before they get better! We anticipate a quick resolution of the problem. Instead, the problem becomes magnified. Like Moses, we are tempted to doubt the word God gave us. Parents who pray afresh for a wayward daughter are crushed when her behavior worsens. A pastor who seeks God to revive his church is dismayed when his godly efforts yield criticism instead of contrition. Folks who prayerfully adopt a destitute child encounter medical or emotional problems they never saw coming. Often, standing on God's promises involves more than we bargained for.

> After we pray or step out in obedience, things may get worse before they get better!

When the Hebrew foremen protested Pharaoh's unfair labor practices, they were thrown out of his palace. Instead of running to Moses to ask for help, they let him have it:

> "May the LORD look upon you and judge you! You have made us a stench to Pharaoh and his officials and have put a sword in their hand to kill us" (Exodus 5:21).

Trusting in the Lord did not make Moses' life easier but instead placed him on a spiritual and emotional roller coaster. The Hebrews who had bowed in worship when they first heard God's message now wished they had never encouraged their emancipator. Instead they blamed him for a new load of hardships. All of this was too much for Moses, who asked God,

> "O Lord, why have you brought trouble upon this people? Is this why you sent me? Ever since I went to Pharaoh to speak in your name, he has brought trouble upon this people, and you have not rescued your people at all" (Exodus 5:22–23).

Bewilderment and discouragement overwhelmed the servant of God. The word Moses received out of the burning bush had not come to pass. What exactly was going on? Hadn't he obeyed God's instructions? Where was the promised deliverance? Moses couldn't deny that God had spoken to him, but the word of the Lord was sorely testing him.

Like Moses, we must go through the same process if we want to walk and pray in faith. Like him, we need to cling to the word of the Lord despite the negative circumstances we see around us.

Remember young Joseph with his dreams from God? Talk about a roller coaster ride! Joseph was prophetically destined for a position of distinguished leadership, but his jealous brothers tried to kill him and then sold him to slave traders heading toward Egypt. Then a leading Egyptian put Joseph to work in his house and things seemed brighter. But soon the man's wife brought slanderous charges against Joseph that landed him in prison. How could those dreams come true now? Where was God, who had intimated that Joseph would one day rise to such a great height that even his family would bow before him? As Joseph paced around his prison cell, voices of mocking unbelief must have attacked his soul: "Look at what you foolishly believed and see where you have ended up!"

The Psalms talk about the life of Joseph:

> They afflicted his feet with fetters,
> He himself was laid in irons;
> Until the time that his word came to pass,
> *The word of the LORD tested him*
> (Psalm 105:18–19 NASB).

In what way did the "word of the Lord" *test* Joseph? The Hebrew word used here speaks of refining metals to remove impurities. As Joseph lay rotting in prison, God's word had a purging effect on him. Would he continue to trust and worship despite his circumstances, or would he give in to despair? This is how God's Word refines all of us. We act on his promise, and the testing begins. Things turn worse instead of better. Opposition springs up against us. God doesn't seem to hear our prayers. Discouragement leaves us susceptible to temptation.

> Many breakthroughs are not instantaneous. Instead, they place us in the refiner's fire.

This purging process rids us of self-dependence so that our faith can remain solely in God. It refines us of self-indulgence so we can walk in holiness. It deepens our surrender to God's will in preference to other more convenient options. And the experience reminds us that God's grace is sufficient as we wait for the fulfillment of his word. We must accept that many breakthroughs are not instantaneous. Instead, they place us in the refiner's fire. Yet the

Lord's purpose is not to diminish but to abundantly bless us in the end!

> For you, O God, tested us;
>> you refined us like silver.
> You brought us into prison
>> and laid burdens on our backs.
> You let men ride over our heads;
>> we went through fire and water,
>> *but you brought us to a place of abundance*
>> (Psalm 66:10–12).

Why does God sometimes permit his people to go through "fire and water"? Because he wants to enlarge our lives through his purging process. He uses delays, negative circumstances, unfair treatment, and a host of other difficulties as his word works within us. How else can he secure our total trust and surrender than by the process of refining us like silver? So hold on to what God has said even though ten thousand voices tell you it's useless. Move ahead in the assignment he gave you even when you face obstacles on every hand. Never mind how difficult things are for the moment. In just a little while, God will bring you into "a place of abundance."

THE WORD FULFILLED

God will manifest his power on behalf of anyone who comes through the same process that tested Joseph and Moses.

> Then the LORD said to Moses, "*Now* you will see what I will do to Pharaoh: Because of my mighty hand he will

let them go; because of my mighty hand he will drive them out of his country" (Exodus 6:1).

For a time, Moses met with distrust and accusations from his own people, but *now* God will exalt him as their deliverer. For a while Pharaoh controlled events, but *now* the Lord will use his servant to bring an entire nation to its knees. When we hold on to God's word, we will always witness a day when the Lord says, "*Now* you will see what I will do!" The testing of God's word is always followed by the fulfillment of it.

STEPPING OUT

In chapter 5, I told the story of a young woman named Farah, whom the Lord rescued from her own "Egypt." Farah's life has been turned around because of a wonderful Christian ministry in New Hampshire dedicated to helping hurting women and their children. I couldn't help but wonder what would have happened to Farah if New Life hadn't taken her in. What if there had never been a New Life at all? This unusual ministry was started more than twenty-five years ago by a couple who know firsthand how the word of the Lord can test and purify our faith.

Grace Rosado grew up in a strict Italian family just outside Boston. Her father was a faithful man of God and the pastor of an ethnic Italian church. When she was in high school, Grace attended a service one evening where former drug addicts gave testimony to the liberating power of Jesus Christ. That night she wept like a baby and felt determined to help men trapped in the vicious world of drug abuse.

Young Grace couldn't wait to tell her father she had found her calling. But the man who had helped nourish her faith was far too conservative to rejoice at the news that his daughter wanted to enter such an unsavory world. Though he did what he could to discourage her, Grace persisted, and at age seventeen she took the bold step of applying for a job at the local Teen Challenge, a Christian ministry for men needing rehabilitation and discipleship. A sheltered young woman without experience, she had every reason to be nervous. She was disappointed to be told there were no openings for her to work with men who were addicted to drugs—but then learned that Teen Challenge was opening a new women's program that very day. The new director desperately needed an assistant. Grace walked right through the door the Lord had opened.

After nearly two years of working in the women's program, Grace went off to Bible school, along with her boyfriend, who had also been on staff at Teen Challenge. After graduation, Grace and George married and settled down in Massachusetts, where they got jobs and began serving the Lord at a local church. But Grace's dream of helping the desperate was still alive in her heart.

The young couple had friends who operated a ministry for troubled women in another state. When Grace and George asked them to consider opening such a ministry in New England, the response shocked them: "Why don't you begin a program, since God gave you the burden?"

Though both had worked for a ministry, they had never considered starting one. After all, they had neither money nor connections, and they were still quite young. But as they prayed and talked, they became convinced God had indeed given them this burden for a reason. Even so, how and where should they begin? They knew that troubled girls would need a safe, loving environment in which to respond to the gospel. Yet, with no money it seemed impossible to secure such a place.

Since they were sure God was leading them, they began visiting churches throughout New England to share their dream. Though potential donors were stirred by their vision of helping the lowest of the low, they always heard the same thing: "Come back and see us when you have a house with girls living in it." But the two barely had gas money for the trip back home. How could they purchase the large house they needed?

After checking real estate listings for several months, George came across an interesting property involving a large house on thirty-two acres. It was in tiny Chester, New Hampshire (pop. 1,600), and the listing indicated it was offered as a lease with an option to buy. Even though they had no money, Grace and George made the trip north. They were puzzled, though, when the real estate agent declined to take them to the house, saying, "The doors are open—go see it for yourselves."

While her husband drove the car, Grace silently prayed for God's direction. As she did, she felt a deep peace that this was the property the Lord had for them. But her conviction was severely tested the moment she stepped into the house. The door was open all right, and the house smelled as if every animal in the surrounding woods had lived there at one time or another. George wanted to turn around and leave, but Grace persuaded him to do a walk-through.

> Though the rugs were horribly stained, with garbage strewn everywhere, Grace saw the house with eyes of faith.

Though the rugs were horribly stained, with garbage strewn everywhere, Grace saw the house with eyes of faith. God could use this place for his glory—she was certain of it. Before long, George began to see it, too.

The local businessman who owned the property had two other offers pending but promised to prepare papers as long as they could deliver a check for $1,500 by the following Monday. It was Friday afternoon. Where would they get the money? Still they clung to God's word as they drove home that evening.

The next day Grace and George met with another businessman, keeping an appointment they had previously scheduled. They were shocked when the man handed them a check for $1,000! That Sunday, George had a speaking commitment at a nearby church. After the service a lady approached him, telling him she had just received an inheritance. The Lord had spoken to her and she wanted to give a tithe of it to this ministry for troubled girls. She then handed him a check for $500. In just two days they had the exact amount of money they needed.

Of course, that was just the beginning of their roller coaster ride of faith. But through all the ups and downs, as they set about cleaning up, renovating, and furnishing the house and then learning to run the new ministry, the Lord was always there providing for their needs. One thing they never lacked was hurting women in need of God's help.

Years later, the two again stepped out in faith. It was one thing to accept women without children but another thing entirely to accept women *with* their children. Opening their doors even wider meant holding on tighter to the promise God had given them. Yet the One who began the work has never failed. For more than twenty-five years the staff of New Life have been trusting God, and he has continued to supply all their needs.

Some very tough women have ended up at New Life. Many wear their anger on their faces and bear terrible scars in their souls from the ravages of sin and abuse. All are welcomed by the once-sheltered girl who received a burden from the Lord years ago. No matter how hardened or hopeless they seem on the outside, Grace Rosado knows how beautiful they can become as Jesus begins his work in them. "Therefore, if anyone is in Christ, he is a new creation; the old has gone, the new has come!" (2 Corinthians 5:17).

CHAPTER EIGHT

A BREAK-
THROUGH
Moment

*A*lthough it's crucial to understand the principles
governing prayer, understanding alone won't
lead you to a breakthrough. In fact, prayerlessness often co-
exists with extensive Bible knowledge. Only the Holy Spirit
can inspire us to pray effectually, and he uses various means
to accomplish his purpose.

First of all, serious prayer is born out of a sense of need,
out of the knowledge that we must ask God to intervene.
The Spirit of God moves us toward prayer by using Scripture to show us two things: our human need and the Lord's
promise of provision. Breakthrough prayer isn't born out
of an "I should pray today" attitude but, instead, out of
an "I must have God's help" frame of mind. Many times I
have heard sermons that convicted me to the point where

I *had* to pray even though the message itself said nothing about asking and receiving from God. Self-satisfied believers cannot, by definition, experience the true spirit of prayer.

CONTAGIOUS PRAYER

Like worship and hunger for God, the impulse to pray is often contagious. We catch it as we watch others presenting their needs at the throne of grace, pouring their souls out in prayer. Years ago I reached one of the lowest points in my spiritual life. I was so challenged by the ministry and so discouraged that I felt dangerously numb. The Lord seemed remote, too distant to help me, and I fell into a depressed, prayerless state. All of this happened while I was trying to pastor a church!

One Sunday during a time of prayer, I noticed a woman standing at the edge of the platform, sobbing quietly and then gradually raising her hands toward heaven. Her uplifted face, stained with tears, reflected the earnestness of her heart. In her, I saw my answer. The God she was imploring was the same one I needed to call on. I broke down in tears and began seeking the Lord again. God used that woman to encourage a pastor in spiritual trouble, though not one word ever passed between us. That night I found the strength to continue my journey.

This was not a case of emotional excess, but an example of how the act of prayer itself can inspire others. I never learned that woman's name, but another one named Hannah, whose story is told in the Bible, has also provided motivation for my prayer life.

BREAKING POINTS

Hannah could be called "the First Lady of Prayer" because she's the first woman whose petition is recorded in Scripture. Her story is related in some detail, showing us how God uses deep human need as a springboard to accomplish his purposes. Whenever he does this, believers receive answers they can hardly believe.

> God uses deep human need as a springboard to accomplish his purposes. Whenever he does this, believers receive answers they can hardly believe.

Hannah lived in Israel during an era of great lawlessness, a time when no king ruled and "everyone did as he saw fit" (Judges 21:25). To make matters worse, she shared her husband, Elkanah, with an unpleasant woman named Peninnah, who was his second wife. Hannah's inability to have children made her the constant brunt of Peninnah's taunts.

> Year after year this man [Elkanah] went up from his town to worship and sacrifice to the LORD Almighty at Shiloh.... Whenever the day came for Elkanah to sacrifice, he would give portions of the meat to his wife Peninnah and to all her sons and daughters. But to Hannah he gave a double portion because he loved her, and the LORD had closed her womb. And because the LORD had closed her womb, her rival kept provoking her in order to irritate her. This went on year after year. Whenever Hannah went up to the house of the LORD, her rival provoked her till she wept and would not eat (1 Samuel 1:3–7).

Constantly tormented, with no offspring of her own, weeping and unable to eat, Hannah seemed mired in a hopeless situation. In the midst of her pain, she didn't know what God was about to do. She had no idea that he was going to raise up a prophet who would lead his wayward people back to himself. Nor did she know that God would choose her, among all the women of Israel, to bear that child. God chose this heartbroken woman out of compassion and grace. And he used a remarkable method to bring about the birth of Hannah's son, Samuel.

> Once when they had finished eating and drinking in Shiloh, Hannah stood up. Now Eli the priest was sitting on a chair by the doorpost of the LORD's temple. In bitterness of soul Hannah wept much and prayed to the LORD. And she made a vow, saying, "O LORD Almighty, if you will only look upon your servant's misery and remember me, and not forget your servant but give her a son, then I will give him to the LORD for all the days of his life" (1 Samuel 1:9–11).

This prayer, one of the greatest in the Bible, not only changed Hannah's life, but also altered the history of Israel. Scripture doesn't say what finally drove Hannah to stand and pray that day, but it led to a breakthrough moment with God. This is the process the Lord often uses—working out his plans through weak human beings who feel compelled by their need to pray.

Incredibly, we have the same potential in prayer that Hannah did. Like Hannah, our "breaking point" can lead to a "breakthrough" if it spurs us to call on God. Hannah asked for a son, but God gave her much more. The long, depressing cycle that had continued year after year was broken in just a few moments spent with God. The same can be true for us today because we pray to the same God Hannah prayed to—an unchanging God.

PRAYING FROM YOUR HEART

Hannah's encounter with the Lord was not about emotional fanaticism. Her example assures us that a prayer-answering God can resolve seemingly hopeless situations. If we deny or doubt that fact, we are the losers. Many times, sons and daughters are wooed back to the Lord through a mom or dad breaking through in prayer. Great things still happen when we follow Hannah's example and appeal to the Lord.

Hannah's sorrow, tears, and anguish showed the earnestness and intensity of her petition. Rather than offering a superficial prayer, she prayed from her heart's deepest desire. It is tragic that heartfelt prayer is out of style in many churches because of a strong need to keep things decent and orderly. Of course, we should avoid shallow emotionalism, but we needn't throw out the baby with the bath water.

There is no reason to think that only quiet, controlled prayer is acceptable. Jesus knew what he was doing when "he offered up prayers and petitions with loud cries and tears to the one who could save him" (Hebrews 5:7). If Jesus, the Son of God, sometimes prayed like that, why shouldn't we? Many churches and denominations have become so lukewarm that they've produced teaching that reflects their own spiritual condition rather than the truth of the Bible. If a person never shows emotion, we know that something is wrong, that some kind of emotional or physical problem is at work. Similarly, a complete lack of emotion in prayer is a sign of a spiritual ailment.

There is no reason to think that only quiet, controlled prayer is acceptable. If Jesus, the Son of God, sometimes prayed "with loud cries and tears," why shouldn't we?

People pour out their souls to God in various ways. In Hannah's case, her distress at one point was expressed without words.

> As she kept on praying to the LORD, Eli observed her mouth. Hannah was praying in her heart, and her lips were moving but her voice was not heard (1 Samuel 1:12–13).

Like Hannah, we sometimes find it difficult to form the proper words for prayer. But God hears our heart's cry even when our mouths are silent. Hannah's tears spoke more profoundly than words, and she found favor with the Lord.

SPIRITUAL OPPOSITION

Not everyone was impressed by Hannah's earnest prayer. Sadly, Hannah was misunderstood and opposed by a man who should have known better.

> Eli thought she was drunk and said to her, "How long will you keep on getting drunk? Get rid of your wine."
> "Not so, my lord," Hannah replied, "I am a woman who is deeply troubled. I have not been drinking wine or beer; I was pouring out my soul to the LORD. Do not take your servant for a wicked woman; I have been praying here out of my great anguish and grief" (1 Samuel 1:13–16).

The high priest, Eli, had grown so spiritually insensitive that he couldn't tell the difference between prayer and a drunken stupor. Fortunately, Hannah didn't react with anger or lose the spirit of prayer. Her experience at this moment points to an important lesson about prayer: If you pray, you will certainly become a target of Satan, who will immediately attack you with spiritual opposition and discouragement. The secret to prevailing in prayer involves "pressing through" and "holding on to God." Don't be distracted when people accuse you of fanaticism because you believe God answers prayer. Follow the Spirit's leading and ignore everything that discourages you from trusting the Lord.

> If you pray, you will certainly become a target of Satan, who will immediately attack you with spiritual opposition and discouragement.

"PRAYING THROUGH"

After Hannah explained to Eli what was really happening, she manifested great faith in God. "Eli answered, 'Go in peace, and may the God of Israel grant you what you have asked of him'" (1 Samuel 1:17). Upon hearing that word from the priest of God, Hannah "went her way and ate something, and her face was no longer downcast" (v. 18).

Even while Hannah had been praying, her tears had stopped flowing because she felt sure her petition would be granted. She left for home the next day, and soon after, she conceived a child by her husband, Elkanah. Hannah was sure about God's answer *before* she conceived her child.

Hannah's experience highlights one of the unique blessings of breakthrough prayer. The Spirit of God is able to grant a profound inner assurance that what we have asked for has been granted. Some earlier Christians used the term "praying through" to describe the supplication that stays at the throne of grace until this assurance has been granted. Rather than the human-centered "name it and claim it" formula, this is the "pray it and know it" cycle that comes from the Holy Spirit.

Some problems, of course, will not be resolved by a few moments spent in heartfelt prayer. These can only be overcome by extended times of prayer and waiting in faith. To contend otherwise is to fly in the face of God's Word. Paul understood this in giving instructions about spiritual warfare in his letter to the Ephesians:

> Pray in the Spirit on all occasions with all kinds of prayers and requests. With this in mind, be alert and always keep on praying for all the saints. Pray also for me, that whenever I open my mouth, words may be given me. . . . Pray that I may declare [the gospel] fearlessly, as I should (Ephesians 6:18–20).

Why must there be "all kinds of prayer" on "all occasions" if God has already decided to help us? Why must we "keep on praying for all the saints" if one concise petition can do the trick? Why does Paul entreat others to pray for him? Why should the church in Ephesus pray for boldness in his preaching when all Paul needs to do is "name it and claim it"?

These are some of the mysteries of prayer that God never fully explains. Still, he gives spiritual insight to those who spend time with him at the throne of grace. We desperately need churches and individuals who will pray on all occasions, with all kinds of prayer and supplication. If we do our part, God will do his.

ANOTHER SECRET OF PRAYER

Hannah did something else that day in the temple that shows us how to succeed in prayer. She dedicated the son she prayed for before he was even conceived. Her request included this pledge: "Then I will give him to the LORD for all the days of his life" (1 Samuel 1:11). It seems at first glance as though she was bargaining with God, but that wasn't so. Hannah asked for a son and promised God that the answer would be consecrated to him. Mixed with her desire for a child was a desire to extol the name of the Lord.

A common problem in our prayer is that we focus only on ourselves with little thought to how God can be glorified. Paul tells us that the blessings of redemption through Christ are not merely for our benefit, but more essentially for "the praise of his glorious grace" (Ephesians 1:6). So it is with answers to prayer. We should pray for spiritual renewal across the land not so much for the blessings it will bring us, but so that God's name may be exalted.

Hannah received her answer, only to give her son up for the service and glory of God. To fulfill her pledge she eventually left young Samuel to be raised in the house of the Lord in Shiloh. But you needn't feel sorry for her, because there's more to the story.

The LORD was gracious to Hannah; she conceived and gave birth to three sons and two daughters. Meanwhile, the boy Samuel grew up in the presence of the LORD (1 Samuel 2:21).

That day in the temple, Hannah had risen to pray even though she was weighed down with distress. But in the end, God weighed her down with children. She had five kids at home as well as a son in Shiloh who would one day lead Israel. Like Hannah, we always win when we live for the glory of God.

PRAYER BRINGS PEACE

Hannah's prayer is outstanding in yet another way because it powerfully illustrates how prayer relieves the soul of the burdens it carries. Most Christians can quote from memory the Bible verse, "Cast all your anxiety on him because he cares for you" (1 Peter 5:7). But reciting a verse is different from putting it into practice. Putting the verse into practice means unloading our burdens through fervent prayer. Hannah transferred the weight of her burdens onto the Lord that day in Shiloh. She left for home "lighter" and filled with peace.

When God's choicest saints felt overwhelmed by their circumstances, they found relief the same way Hannah did—by converting their troubles into a cry for help to God.

> Yet I am poor and needy;
>> may the Lord think of me.
> You are my help and my deliverer;
>> O my God, do not delay (Psalm 40:17).

David combined *faith* in God's character with a *prayer* for help. The actual transfer of our anxiety, fear, or sorrow occurs when we give it to God *in prayer.* Lack of prayer translates into lack of peace no matter how knowledgeable we are about the Bible. Countless Christians are living with unnecessary anxiety even though they regularly hear biblical sermons and read sound spiritual literature. God's invitation is not so much to "read all about it" but rather to call on him.

> Lack of prayer translates into lack of peace no matter how knowledgeable we are about the Bible.

God is deeply concerned when his children are burdened by anxiety, in much the way parents are concerned about their children. It is tragic that we often worry ourselves to death when God's supernatural peace is only a prayer away.

> *Do not be anxious about anything,* but in *everything,* by prayer and petition, with thanksgiving, *present your requests to God.* And *the peace of God,* which transcends all understanding, *will guard* your hearts and your minds in Christ Jesus (Philippians 4:6–7).

In a world filled with problems and pain, the Lord has promised peace when we pray. No sweeter promise can be found in the Bible. The temptation toward anxiety is assumed, but a place of relief is provided—the throne of grace. God's unique 24/7 security system is available for both heart and mind *if* we pour out our hearts to him in prayer. If we don't, we will continue to trudge despondently through life with only ourselves to blame. It's true that regular praying costs something, but the cost of not praying is much higher.

VIVIAN'S STORY

As I picture Hannah happily returning home from her meeting with God, I think of another young woman, who was also overwhelmed by years of accumulated pain. If you saw her smiling face in the front row of the Brooklyn Tabernacle Choir, you would never imagine the breakthrough moment that saved her life. Her name is Vivian, and her story begins in Guyana, South America, where she was born.

"The population of the little town where I was born was entirely Indian. My parents were devout Hindus, as was most everyone else. There was one tiny Christian church in town, but we were warned never to go near it because it was 'haunted.' My dad died when I was only a year-and-a-half old, leaving my mother alone to care for me and my older brother.

"I vividly remember praying at the altar in the Hindu temple, singing in the choir, and faithfully observing each holiday. It helped fill the void I felt after my mom left for America when I was only three. I knew she hoped to find work so she could bring my brother and me there one day, but I felt so alone without her. My religious instincts were soon eclipsed by a sense of depression and emptiness unusual for someone so young.

"A strange memory from those years still lingers. Walking by a stream one day, I saw new Christians being baptized and longed to share in the joy they were experiencing.

"Finally, when I was ten, my brother and I joined my mother in New York. After a few years, I stopped practicing Hindu rituals because they seemed so useless. About that time, my home life became a nightmare. Suddenly, my mother and brother both turned on me, though I had no idea why. Both abused me verbally because of their anger and inner turmoil. My brother took it a step further by punching and choking me. I felt terribly confused, hurt, and alone. To escape all the cursing, yelling, and abuse, I even tried drowning myself once in the bathtub.

"A strange memory still lingers. I saw new Christians being baptized and longed to share in the joy they were experiencing."

"When I reached high school, I discovered something that helped me forget—boys. Before long, my brother began monitoring my phone calls, and he and my mother began calling me a whore. I slept with my first real boyfriend when I was sixteen, only to have him reject me soon after. That was the start of what became a long and hopeless cycle: giving myself physically, hoping the next guy would be 'the one,' and then ending up feeling used.

"After a while, to help myself loosen up, I started drinking and smoking pot. One night, two 'friends' took advantage of my condition by raping me. Then they dumped me on a deserted street in a strange neighborhood. After that,

I didn't want to live anymore. Still, I kept looking for someone who could make me happy.

"Despite the roller coaster ride I was on, my grades in school were excellent. I even entered a special program enabling me to graduate a year earlier than scheduled. That was fine by me, since I wanted to go to college to get away from home. Then I met Luis. He had immense charm, and I fell madly in love even though he didn't hide his criminal record or his membership in the Latin Kings. I was so naïve, not realizing they were a highly organized gang involved in big-time crime.

"Though we assured each other of our love, ours was a rocky relationship from the start. Whenever we broke up, I felt miserable. No amount of night-clubbing or fooling around could make me stop wanting to be with him. I tried anything in order to cope with the loneliness I felt when we were apart.

"One summer I dabbled again in Hinduism, this time at my brother's urging. He had really gotten into it and invited me to practice yoga meditation along with him. Once while meditating, I slipped into a kind of trance in which I saw a horrible face that threatened to either suffocate or enter me. I came out of it, but was deeply shaken. From then on, I became convinced that Hinduism's 'out-of-body travel' was not the answer I needed.

"No one had ever told me about Jesus' love or about his power to lift me from the pit of pain I was living in."

"Then I heard devastating news. Luis had been arrested for murder, along with some of his friends. He told me it was an accident, but it soon came out that he had pulled the trigger. Realizing he would spend years behind bars, my world came crashing down. That's when I wrote a suicide note, planning to jump out the window of my college dorm. A friend talked me out of it before I had the chance. But feelings of worthlessness and despair tormented me.

"That's when an acquaintance invited me to visit a church called the Brooklyn Tabernacle. Because I felt that some kind of religious ceremony might help me, I agreed to go. When the pastor gave the message, I realized I had never heard about the Jesus of the Bible. No one had ever told me about his love or about his power to lift me from the pit of pain I was living in. I had always thought religion was about traditions and ceremonies and rules that must be obeyed. I had no idea God could wash away the dirt of my sin and send the Holy Spirit to live in me.

"When the pastor asked people to come forward to pray and invite Christ into their hearts, I was among the first to rise from my seat. Oh, how Jesus met me that day as I gave him my sins, my problems, and my life! The peace I had been searching for was finally mine, along with a joy I can't even explain. It just filled me up. A life that was empty and so hurt has now become the place where Jesus lives."

Vivian rose up that day to pray, just as Hannah had risen up so long ago. The same God who had heard and answered the desperate prayer of a barren woman heard the prayer of a spiritually empty young woman whose life was spiraling downward. Like Hannah, Vivian stood up and experienced her own breakthrough moment of prayer. And the Lord supplied her need, filling her with joy and a deep peace about the future.

Why should any of us wait one more minute to receive what we need from God? Let this be our day to arise and talk to the Father from our hearts. Let this be our day to experience a breakthrough moment in which we will receive help through the loving power of our prayer-answering God.

CHAPTER NINE

BREAK THROUGH
to Holiness

*O*ld Eli, the priest Hannah had encountered in the temple at Shiloh, sat in a chair by the side of the road waiting for news. Four thousand Israelites had recently been slaughtered by the Philistine army. Eli's sons, Hophni and Phinehas, priests like him, had hurried to the Israelite camp, taking with them the ark of the covenant, hoping it would turn the tide of battle. Fearing for the ark, the old priest leaned forward in his seat as soon as he heard someone running toward the city gate. The messenger was battered and worn, his clothes torn and dirty. He doubled over, breathing hard before standing again to deliver the news.

"I have just come from the battle line: I fled from it this very day."

"What happened, my son?" Eli asked.

"Israel fled before the Philistines, and the army has suffered heavy losses."

The young man lowered his eyes, speaking more slowly now to give the old man time to react: "Your two sons, Hophni and Phinehas, are dead." And then, with hesitation, came the worst news of all: "The ark of God has been captured."

As soon as Eli heard that the ark had fallen into enemy hands, he pitched backward off his chair, breaking his neck. The ninety-eight-year-old priest who had led Israel for forty years was dead.

Like the whirlpool created by a ship's sinking, the news spread rapidly through Shiloh, pulling others into despair. When Eli's daughter-in-law, the wife of Phinehas, heard what had happened, she went into early labor. Overcome by pain, she refused to be comforted by the news that she had given birth to a son. As she lay dying, she named her child Ichabod, meaning "no glory," and pronounced the truth everyone already knew: "The glory has departed from Israel, for the ark of God has been captured." (See 1 Samuel 4:12–22.)

How was it that God's covenant people had been forced to retreat from their enemies, the idolatrous Philistines? Why did their soldiers die when the Lord was supposed to have been on their side? How could God permit his own high priest and his two sons to die on the very same day? And finally, why was the ark of the covenant, symbolizing the uniqueness of Israel, now in enemy hands? The answer to all these questions is simply this: Divine judgment had fallen on God's own people. The Lord was cleaning house.

WHEN THINGS GET MESSY

Sometimes things get so messy that the only solution is to undertake a total house cleaning. That's certainly true of corporate restructuring, but it's also true of God's way of governing his people. Situations can become so intolerable that the Lord must take drastic action to protect the future blessing of his children. Admittedly, this is a "breakthrough" of a different kind, but one that is absolutely essential if we are to experience real power in prayer.

To understand the sad turn of events in Israel's history we must keep in mind one of the first principles of the spiritual life. Paul wrote about this in his letter to the Galatians: "Do not be deceived: God cannot be mocked. A man reaps what he sows" (6:7).

It didn't matter that Israel was God's chosen people. If anything, their special status made their situation worse because of the tremendous privilege they had been given. They had the light of Scripture; they were Abraham's offspring; they had received the law God had entrusted to Moses; they understood the blood sacrifice basis of approaching God. And still they were faithless, turning away from the Lord.

> Situations can become so intolerable that the Lord must take drastic action to protect the future blessing of his children.

The Bible describes Eli's sons, the priests Hophni and Phinehas, in no uncertain terms. They were worthless scoundrels who did not even know the Lord. Instead of honoring God by performing the offerings as prescribed, they greedily demanded the best meat for themselves, thus holding God in contempt (1 Samuel 2:12–17).

Sadly, there was much more to the priests' sins than greed. "Now Eli, who was very old, heard about everything his sons were doing to all Israel and how they slept with the women who served at the entrance to the Tent of Meeting" (v. 22).

Hophni and Phinehas were taking advantage of the women who worked in the precincts of the Tabernacle. Incredibly, the two expressed neither shame nor repentance about their conduct. They may even have told the women that their exalted position gave them license to live above the moral laws God had for everyone else. After all, they were priests of the Most High with daily access to the Holy Place just inside the veil that led to God's Holy of Holies!

Month after month and year after year, the Lord permitted this ungodliness in his own Tabernacle. No lightning bolt flashed out of heaven to destroy the two priests, and for a while it seemed their treachery would go unpunished.

But all the while that Hophni and Phinehas were working their scam against the people, God was working on a solution in the shape of a small boy who was faithfully serving him right under their noses. While they pursued their selfish passions, this boy performed his daily ministry to the Lord, wearing a simple linen garment symbolizing his purity and devotion. Hannah's son Samuel, the one who had been the answer to her prayer for a child, was growing up in the temple at Shiloh.

God had arranged it so that Samuel would be ready to lead Israel after Eli and his wicked sons died. What an incredible Old Testament picture of the wheat and weeds growing up together! Whenever God orchestrates a changing of the guard, he replaces unholy conduct with godly living.

THE MONEY TREE

On a recent visit, a friend who's a well-known gospel music artist filled me in on some new fundraising methods cropping up in various church circles. I already knew about the shady gimmicks and dishonest techniques that are sometimes used to separate God's people from their money. I knew all about "seed faith" teachers who take Scripture out of context to guarantee you will reap a blessing if you support their ministries. These practices are far from the ministry model given us by the apostle Paul: "Surely you remember, brothers, our toil and hardship; *we worked night and day in order not to be a burden to anyone* while we preached the gospel of God to you" (1 Thessalonians 2:9).

When those in ministry follow the footsteps of Jesus, their goal is to pour themselves out sacrificially for others, not to amass large personal fortunes. We know that the temptation to profit from ministry was a problem in Paul's time, because he spoke of it when writing to the Christians in Corinth: "Unlike so many, we *do not peddle the word of God for profit*" (2 Corinthians 2:17).

But, no, these weren't the scams my friend was talking about. One of the hottest new ministries around, he told me, is based on chanting, praying, and mentally imaging that "money is on its way." Never mind if you have a relationship with God or whether you are living in sin. Never mind about following the will of God, displaying the fruits of the Spirit, or influencing souls for Christ. In the end, it's all about money. You commonly hear whole sermons today about nothing but money. In some churches the meaning of the cross, the power of the Spirit, the preeminence of love, and other great themes of Scripture are hardly mentioned unless they can be linked to the money tree.

> In some churches the meaning of the cross and other great themes of Scripture are hardly mentioned unless they can be linked to the money tree.

But there was more. Hadn't I heard about "giving into your new level of anointing"? Certain churches teach people to leave their seats as soon as a preacher or singer reaches a high level of "anointing." They are to rush down with their offering for "God's servant." Unless they do, they will never reach that "higher place" God has ordained for them. Can you picture Jesus or Paul or Peter or John involved in such business? These money-loving preachers are laughing all the way to the bank, heedless of the fact that God will clean house as surely as he did in the days of Hophni and Phinehas.

ALL IS NOT WELL

Applying this portion of Scripture to our day is a delicate matter. My purpose is to be neither sensational nor judgmental. Yet those who love Christ and his Word cannot ignore contemporary trends that pose ominous threats to the purity of his body, the church. Here are a few of the signs that all is not right with the body of Christ. None of us can afford to ignore them, nor can we write them off as problems that will never confront our own churches. Instead, we need to be vigilant and quick to repent and reform should the need arise.

Who is not aware of the sex-abuse scandal among Roman Catholic priests that has shaken the confidence of people in all clergymen? Because those in authority often "looked the other way," as Eli did with his sons, predators were allowed to continue harming innocent children. This terrible evil has been sadly linked with the words *Christian* and *church*.

In other circles there is a plague of divorce and remarriage among high-profile ministers. One minister, who gained a divorce without biblical grounds and then quickly remarried, claimed to an applauding congregation that his "anointing was now stronger" as a result of his actions! Many such ministers who continue preaching in churches and on television without a pause are terrible representatives of the God who declared, "I hate divorce" (Malachi 2:16).

Consider, too, the problem of homosexuality within the church. A pastor I know could no longer ignore the obvious fact that church leaders were condoning the behavior of practicing homosexuals in the congregation. Because my friend couldn't reconcile this behavior with his Bible, he left that church. Unfortunately, his experience is not unique.

Whose heart is not broken at the thought of parents who faithfully bring their children to God's house only to see them initiated into unholy things?

Why do church leaders tolerate such practices? Sometimes it's a matter of keeping attendance up, maintaining musical excellence, or fattening the church's purse. But such failures in leadership have grieved the Spirit who is called "Holy" and whose power and presence have been withdrawn from the life of their congregations. Although leaders can use emotionalism, hype, and distorted interpretations of Scripture to try to cover up this reality, God's Word is crystal clear:

> Do not be deceived: Neither the sexually immoral nor idolaters nor adulterers nor male prostitutes nor homosexual offenders ... will inherit the kingdom of God (1 Corinthians 6:9–10).

Fortunately, God shows mercy to each of us when we repent, no matter the sin. Without his forgiveness, where would any of us be? Yet people who profess faith in God while unrepentantly practicing iniquity will eventually be condemned as were Hophni and Phinehas.

Less shocking but more widespread is the problem of sensuality, which is now accepted among large numbers of believers. Recently a group of gospel artists performed on television while scantily dressed cheerleader-dancers gyrated behind them to the beat of the music. Though their lyrics mentioned God, the atmosphere was sexually charged. Defenders of this kind of "showmanship" rationalize it by saying that performers need to relate to their audience. They feel the need to become liberated from the "uptight standards of an old-fashioned era." One Christian magazine went so far as to report that a certain gospel singer was voted "most sexy" among his peers!

The bottom-line question when it comes to such behavior should not be what we think about it but what God's Holy Spirit thinks about it. All too often, a horrible kind of "reverse conversion" is taking place in which the world and its desires are changing Christians rather than the other way around. Some people seem to have forgotten— or perhaps never learned—that the church was born in a *holy* atmosphere:

> A horrible kind of "reverse conversion" is taking place in which the world is changing Christians rather than the other way around.

> With many other words he warned them; and he pleaded with them, "Save yourselves from *this corrupt generation*" (Acts 2:40).

> "Therefore *come out from them and be separate,* says the Lord. Touch no unclean thing, and I will receive you" (2 Corinthians 6:17).

Christ sent us to convert the world, not be conformed to it. When sensuality is accepted in partnership with the message of the gospel, we are deceived, becoming strangers to the power of God. If the Lord called Peter's generation "corrupt," how would he define America in the twenty-first century? Just because God loves the world doesn't mean he has lost his holy hatred of sin. Let's pray for a spiritual revival that will clean the church of unholy practices!

CROSSING THE LINE

Though Eli was not guilty of the sins of his two sons, he was guilty of failing to take action against them.

So he [Eli] said to them, "Why do you do such things? I hear from all the people about these wicked deeds of yours. No, my sons; it is not a good report I hear spreading among the LORD's people. If a man sins against another man, God may mediate for him; but if a man sins against the LORD, who will intercede for him?" (1 Samuel 2:23–25).

That was all old Eli did despite the grievous nature of their sins. He scolded his erring sons mildly but took no action to remove them from the priesthood. After all, they were *his* boys, and—

—Why be judgmental when only God can judge, right?

—Besides, everyone knows how hard it is for a dad with his kids.

—Anyway, no one's perfect.

—Just think of the scandal for Eli's family if his sons were ousted from the Tabernacle!

So Eli, the high priest, looked the other way, allowing his sons' greed and sexual immorality to go unchecked in the house of the Lord. But even the all-merciful God has a line that cannot be crossed.

Now *a man of God* came to Eli and said to him, "This is what the LORD says: 'Did I not clearly reveal myself to your father's house when they were in Egypt under Pharaoh? I chose your father [Aaron] out of all the tribes of Israel to be my priest, to go up to my altar, to burn incense, and to wear an ephod in my presence.... Why do you scorn my sacrifice and offering that I prescribed for my dwelling? *Why do you honor your sons more than me* by fattening yourselves on the choice parts of every offering made by my people Israel?'" (1 Samuel 2:27–29).

Isn't it wonderful that God still has faithful servants during the darkest spiritual times? An unnamed "man of God" appeared out of nowhere and spoke on behalf of God. Eli's failure to deal with sin in the priesthood had provoked the Lord to anger. The high priest was honoring his sons over God. Isn't it a solemn matter to consider that what some call "tolerance" God judges to be high treason!

WHAT ABOUT GOD'S PROMISES?

The man of God who had spoken to Eli was not yet through:

> "Therefore the LORD, the God of Israel, declares, 'I promised that your house and your father's house would minister before me forever.' But now the LORD declares: 'Far be it from me! *Those who honor me I will honor, but those who despise me will be disdained.* The time is coming when I will cut short your strength and the strength of your father's house, so that there will not be an old man in your family line. . . . And what happens to your two sons, Hophni and Phinehas, will be a sign to you— they will both die on the same day. I will raise up for myself *a faithful priest,* who will do according to what is in my heart and mind'" (1 Samuel 2:30–31, 34–35).

While young Samuel swept the floors in the Tabernacle, God was sweeping his house clean of moral pollution. Even though Eli's family held a promised place of leadership from the Lord, God rescinded their assignment. But doesn't this seem to contradict God's faithfulness to his own promise: "'I promised that your house ... would minister before me forever.' But *now*, ... 'Far be it from me!'" No, because most of the promises found in the Bible are conditional. There are some exceptions, such as the promise that Jesus is coming again, but the great majority of God's promises have conditions attached to them. For example, the Lord has promised wisdom to everyone who asks, but a condition is laid down for successful asking:

> But when he asks, he must believe and not doubt, because he who doubts is like a wave of the sea, blown and tossed by the wind. *That man should not think he will receive anything from the Lord* (James 1:6–7).

Clearly, God promises wisdom to those who ask as long as they ask in faith. In contrast, the Lord hasn't promised anything to those who doubt him as they pray.

The gospel declares that God will grant salvation to every sinner who comes to him as long as they meet his conditions of repentance and faith in Jesus Christ. This is what is meant by the Scripture that describes God as "the Savior of all men, and *especially of those who believe*" (1 Timothy 4:10). Provision has been made for all to be saved, but only those who believe will receive eternal life. Again, we see a definite promise from the Lord that will be fulfilled as long as certain conditions are met.

The fulfillment of God's promises often depends on our walking before him in sincerity and truth.

In the case of Eli and his family, we read of a basic condition that is elsewhere implied in most other divine promises. It is this: God won't be mocked by those who persist in unrighteousness. "Those who honor me I will honor, but those who despise me will be disdained."

The Israelites who came out of Egypt were promised a land flowing with milk and honey, but most of them perished in the desert without seeing it. Their unbelief and rebellion nullified their possession of the land. Likewise, Eli and his sons threw away their blessing from God by their scandalous behavior in Shiloh.

Nothing could be plainer in Scripture than this truth. Unfortunately, some odd theology has produced so-called believers who are totally oblivious to it. Such people walk more in fantasy than in faith, continuing to disobey God while claiming that he will grant the desires of their hearts. After all, they say, "God will be God," and therefore what they do or don't do doesn't matter. Others downplay anything good or bad in human behavior because "God is sovereign and can't be manipulated by his creation." But the episode with Eli's family should convince any unbiased person that the fulfillment of God's promises often depends on our walking before him in sincerity and truth.

No wonder the word of the Lord was rare in those days! No wonder there weren't many visions! It wasn't that God didn't want to communicate with his people. How could he when hardly anyone was listening? The carnality and ungodliness that characterized both priests and people had made them deaf to the voice of the Spirit. That's why Israel was so easily defeated by the Philistine army. That's why the ark of the covenant was captured. God's covenant people were not immune to the law of sowing and reaping.

SPIRITUAL RENEWAL

When the Lord cleans house, he removes those who disrespect him and replaces them with others who revere his name. In contrast to Eli and his sons, Samuel modeled the same deep devotion that had inspired his mother to dedicate her young son to the work of the Lord. Until God stepped in to change things, these opposite attitudes existed together under the same roof. Unholy and holy, dishonor and honor were rubbing shoulders daily in the tabernacle of God.

Jesus warned us that this is always the case. The enemy sows weeds among the wheat so that they grow together in the same field. We can't pull up the weeds lest we pull up the wheat along with them. Yet there will come a day when God cleans house. It could be today or tomorrow or at the final judgment at the end of time:

> "Let both grow together until the harvest. At that time I will tell the harvesters: First collect the weeds and tie them in bundles to be burned; then gather the wheat and bring it into my barn" (Matthew 13:30).

One other change had to be made in the house of the Lord before there could be a breakthrough into holiness in Israel. God needed to find a leader with a listening ear and a sensitive heart so he could communicate with his people. That still needs to happen whenever carnality and arrogance characterize the ministry. The last words in each of

Jesus' letters to the seven churches in the book of Revelation are the same: "He who *has an ear, let him hear what the Spirit says* to the churches" (Revelation 2:7, 11, 17, etc.).

One night when young Samuel was asleep in the Tabernacle, the Lord called to him. Thinking Eli was summoning him, the boy ran to where the high priest slept, but Eli sent Samuel back to his bed. Again the Lord spoke Samuel's name. After a few more mistaken trips, the priest finally discerned that God was doing the calling, and he gave the lad these instructions:

> "Go and lie down, and if he calls you, say, 'Speak, LORD, for your servant is listening.'" So Samuel went and lay down in his place.
>
> The LORD came and stood there, calling as at the other times, "Samuel! Samuel!"
>
> Then Samuel said, "Speak, for your servant is listening" (1 Samuel 3:9–10).

That night a new era began in the history of Israel. After decades of decline and decadence, God had secured a pure, listening heart that could be used to promote spiritual renewal among his people. The days of greedy scams and loose living were coming to an end. Eli and his two sons would soon die—all on the same day—and the Tabernacle would be transformed from a place of profiteering to a house of prayer, as God had always intended it should be.

Don't we need the same kind of housecleaning today? If we really want to pray with power, we need to break through into greater holiness. We don't need a formula or a method for praying. But we do need to live with purity and simplicity rather than with carnality, hype, and hardness as so many in our churches do today.

When Samuel said, "Speak, for your servant is listening," he revealed the secret of what God is after. An attentive, willing heart is the great need of the hour. Programs, talent, and human energy will never accomplish what one man or woman in close fellowship with the living God can do. A young boy in Shiloh led an entire people back from ruin because he was willing to be a humble servant of the great and awesome God.

> An attentive, willing heart is the great need of the hour. Programs will never accomplish what one person in close fellowship with the living God can do.

Today too much of the church suffers from dull, mechanical Bible exposition that lacks the touch of the Holy Spirit. No matter how skilled the preacher, only the Spirit can direct us to the truths that most need to be proclaimed and enable us to apply them in a convicting manner. God is not searching for talent or intelligence on earth, because he is the Almighty One! He already has everything he needs—except our hearts. He wants us to be like Samuel, with a heart that waits to hear and swiftly obey his word. Our present lack of spiritual fruit and power doesn't bring much glory to God. But his answer to our need is always the same:

> Come near to God and he will come near to you.... Humble yourselves before the Lord, and he will lift you up (James 4:8, 10).

Let's ask the Lord to clean his house, beginning with you and me. When our hearts experience a breakthrough, we will find that our prayers are more powerful as well. God has promised to draw near to us with fresh grace *if* we humble ourselves and confess our disobedience. The Lord has never changed, nor will he. Today we can experience a new day of blessing and fruitfulness if we follow Samuel's example by saying with our whole hearts, "Speak, for your servant is listening."

CHAPTER TEN

THE POINT
of Attack

fter hearing reports of new, stubborn influenza strains headed our way last year, I decided to get a flu shot for the first time in my life. I didn't want to become an easy target for the latest virus. I knew that the government monitors the progress of the flu in order to track the most common strains for any particular year. Armed with that knowledge, pharmaceutical companies develop effective vaccines that physicians and clinics then dispense to millions of people across the country, thus helping to thwart a serious epidemic.

This method of fighting the flu is one example of how the medical community battles many diseases. A bacteria or virus poses a physical threat to the region. Doctors understand the problem and prescribe medication or therapy to counteract it. As a result, the entire community is spared the worst effects of an infection or disease that might otherwise run unchecked.

The same procedure works in the spiritual realm, where ministers must often function as doctors of the soul, prescribing the proper biblical remedy to help an ailing patient. And there is no spiritual medicine quite like breakthrough prayer. First, prayer is a tremendous weapon against attacks designed to weaken or destroy what I call our "spiritual immune system." By strengthening our immune system, we can withstand attacks that are designed to destroy our faith and devotion to God. Second, our prayers can bring great encouragement to other Christians who are under siege, helping them break free from discouragement or spiritual stupor, conditions that are often brought on by an attack of the enemy.

OUR SPIRITUAL IMMUNE SYSTEM

The enemy knows that the best way to breach your spiritual immune system is by attacking your faith. Once your faith is undermined, you become an easy target for a variety of spiritual maladies. The apostle Paul was concerned about the spiritual condition of the young church at Thessalonica, a city he was forced to flee because of persecution. Like a spiritual doctor, Paul inquired about the health of the church he planted and then prescribed a biblical remedy for what ailed them.

> So when we could stand it no longer [not being able to see them], we thought it best to be left by ourselves in Athens. We sent Timothy, who is our brother and God's fellow worker in spreading the gospel of Christ, to strengthen and encourage you in your faith, so that no one would be unsettled by these trials. You know quite

well that we were destined for them. In fact, when we were with you, we kept telling you that we would be persecuted. And it turned out that way, as you well know. For this reason, when I could stand it no longer, I sent to find out about your faith. I was afraid that in some way the tempter might have tempted you and our efforts might have been useless (1 Thessalonians 3:1–5).

Separated from his precious spiritual children, Paul sent Timothy to learn about their faith. This was his way of checking the pulse of their spiritual life. Paul wasn't interested in attendance figures or church finances or facilities. He wanted to know about their level of trust in the Lord. Why did the apostle focus on this one aspect of their spiritual life?

Paul knew that faith is paramount in the daily life of the Christian. After all, we are saved by grace through faith. We are admonished to live by faith and not by sight. We are told that without faith it is impossible to please God. Jesus taught that we receive from God according to our faith, and he marveled when he saw great faith. The Bible not only declares that by faith we are justified, but that the righteous

"Justified by faith"
Romans 3:22–26; 5:1

"The righteous will live by faith"
Romans 1:17

"Little faith"
Matthew 6:30; 8:26; 14:31

will live by faith. Christians must daily engage in the good fight of faith but are to remember that through faith they are shielded by God's power.

Paul also knew that personal faith is a living, fluid thing. Scripture speaks of "little" and "great" faith as well as of people who are "full of faith." While some have faith that "is weak," there are Christians whose "faith grows" and even those who "excel in faith." Faith must be "continued in," and it varies in size. (Jesus talks about faith that is "small as a mustard seed.") Most important, there are false doctrines that "destroy the faith of some," and there are Christians who have "shipwrecked their faith." In this context faith means the moral persuasion or conviction that leads the heart to rely on Christ. Because it can grow or diminish, Paul was anxious to know the level of faith among his converts in Thessalonica.

The apostle realized as well that every believer faces difficulties. He didn't want the Thessalonians to be unsettled by their trials, so he reminded them that he had earlier told them they were "destined for them." Paul's Spirit-inspired teaching on this subject is very different from the modern teaching that says "word of faith" people need never experience continued negative circumstances. Paul sent Timothy to see how well the believers at Thessalonica were holding up under ongoing persecution. The Greek word Paul uses for "trials" pictures the pressure that comes from being "crowded or pressed." When Paul said he didn't want the believers to be unsettled, he was using a word that meant "shaken," like the wagging of a dog's tail.

Faith is absolutely essential, not only for spiritual health, but also for breakthrough prayer. James says it is not merely prayer but "the prayer offered in faith" that will make the sick person well (James 5:15). Jesus himself taught plainly that prayer must be combined with faith to secure an answer:

"*If you believe,* you will receive whatever you ask for in prayer" (Matthew 21:22).

When he had gone indoors, the blind men came to him, and he asked them, *"Do you believe that I am able to do this?"* "Yes, Lord," they replied. Then he touched their eyes and said, *"According to your faith* will it be done to you"; and their sight was restored (Matthew 9:28–30).

THE REMEDY

Paul understood the nature of the spiritual conflict facing the converts at Thessalonica and offered a remedy to help them in their trials: "We sent Timothy ... to strengthen and encourage you in your faith." We can make two important deductions from this passage. First, all of us at times need other believers to strengthen and encourage our faith. Second, each of us can at times help other believers by strengthening and encouraging their faith.

The word "strengthen" here means to set fast, to turn resolutely in a certain direction, to fix or confirm. It's the opposite of wavering or drifting. Timothy's task was to steady the faith of the church in Thessalonica, keeping the believers firmly fixed on Jesus despite their trials. He was to remind them that God was still on his throne and that he was allowing these tests to help them mature spiritually. God would somehow use their trials for his glory.

Timothy was not only to strengthen their faith, but also encourage the saints. The word in Greek conveys the idea of exhorting or consoling and is related to the idea of imploring and praying. Prayer was probably one of the ways Timothy encouraged the Thessalonians in the faith.

Spiritual encouragement is not a matter of giving someone a slap on the back or uttering glib phrases such as "keep your chin up." It's about building up our confidence in God. Unless our faith in God grows, we have not helped anyone at the point of attack.

Paul knew that vibrant faith is the critical need of every Christian. A living, growing faith acts as a spiritual immune system, protecting us from spiritual viruses designed by Satan to weaken our life in Christ. Without it, the unthinkable will become thinkable and the unacceptable will become acceptable as we drift away from the safety of life near Jesus. Unfortunately, the spiritual landscape is littered with broken lives that illustrate the dangers of a "sinful, unbelieving heart that turns away from the living God" (Hebrews 3:12). Too many people have made a shipwreck of their faith. Anyone can fall prey to these spiritual maladies if they lack faith. It even happened to an associate of the great apostle Paul, whose name is written in the Holy Bible as a warning to the rest of us: "Demas, because he loved this world, has deserted me and has gone to Thessalonica" (2 Timothy 4:10).

No wonder Paul made encouraging and strengthening believers one of his main priorities. This was his practice after preaching the gospel and founding churches, often in hostile environments:

> Then they returned to Lystra, Iconium and Antioch, *strengthening* the disciples and *encouraging* them to remain true to the faith (Acts 14:21–22).

> So the churches were strengthened in the faith and grew daily in numbers (Acts 16:5).

Paul and his associates weren't handing out vitamin supplements or setting up exercise equipment so the saints could get in shape. Instead, they were strengthening them in their faith because that's what mattered most.

There's a valuable lesson here for us. God, who encourages and strengthens his people, often uses other believers to accomplish his purpose. It wasn't an angel from heaven or a feeling of spiritual ecstasy that fortified the saints in Thessalonica. Instead, the Lord used a young man named Timothy, who later in his life had to be encouraged himself by the apostle Paul (2 Timothy 1:3–10).

What kinds of qualifications are necessary for the indispensable work of faith-building? Paul states, "Therefore *encourage one another* and *build each other up,* just as in fact you are doing" (1 Thessalonians 5:11).

It isn't only pastors and teachers who can boost the faith of struggling Christians. Any of us can minister encouragement if we are sensitive to the needs of others and available to God. The people at Thessalonica understood that they were members of the same body and needed each other.

I have learned that no matter how good someone looks in church on Sunday, you can't tell what kind of battles they may be fighting in the spiritual realm. None of us understand what is really going on behind the smiling faces we see. Many things tend to tear our faith down. It's wonderful when God sends someone to refresh us and strengthen our hold on the Lord. Who knows how things might have turned out for those who have lost faith if only there had been someone like Timothy to encourage them?

THE GIFT OF ENCOURAGING

Of all the gifts of the Holy Spirit, the ministry of encouraging is probably the least appreciated: "We have different gifts, according to the grace given us. If a man's gift is prophesying, let him use it in proportion to his faith. . . . if it is encouraging, let him encourage" (Romans 12:6, 8). We constantly hear about the need for solid teaching and proper leadership in a church, but when was the last time the "gift of encouraging" received its proper due? Our need for it is so acute that the Spirit has granted special grace for some of us to specialize in building people's faith. Just as not all of us are gifted to teach or preach, not everyone has this special anointing to encourage others. Still, we should fervently pray for God to raise up men and women to fulfill this sacred task.

What does this encouragement look like in real life? How is it accomplished? Recently I overheard a woman in a restaurant attempting to comfort a friend who seemed depressed. After listening sympathetically to her list of woes, the woman declared, "You never mind about all that, honey. Just follow your dream, follow your dream!" I doubt that the woman even knew whether her friend had a dream or whether her dream might even have been the source of her problem. Sadly, we live in a day of trite religious slogans and triumphant-sounding phrases that don't really build people up in their faith. Let's analyze some of the ways in which we can strengthen others.

> That is, that you and I may be mutually encouraged by each other's faith (Romans 1:12).

Being strong in the Lord enables us to minister to others who are weak. This is particularly true for encouraging and strengthening someone else's faith. Our own robust faith spills over to lift up those who are struggling. Faith-filled words and actions act as antidotes to the hopelessness people feel when they have lost their grip on God. Sometimes I encounter folks who are so negative and faithless that I feel I need an immediate Bible study or prayer meeting to counter their influence. Such people cause a drain on our spiritual resources. Conversely, it is a real blessing to have fellowship with believers whose faith is so vibrant that it rubs off on me.

> Some folks are so negative and faithless that I feel I need an immediate Bible study or prayer meeting to counter their influence.

ENCOURAGING WORDS

Most often encouragement is conveyed through the words we speak. Consider what Paul says, once again to the Thessalonians: "Therefore encourage each other with these words" (1 Thessalonians 4:18). Paul was referring to the specific words he had just written regarding the truth of Christ's second coming. Like Paul, we can encourage others by sharing the teaching of Scripture and speaking about salvation in Jesus. Remember, "Faith comes from hearing the message" (Romans 10:17). As we speak God's Word, faith can be born in those who hear it. Elsewhere, Paul instructs Titus that church elders should "encourage others by sound doctrine" (Titus 1:9).

Sadly, much of our daily conversation has little real meat in it to edify anyone. Think of the trivial, even foolish subjects that often dominate our thoughts and speech. Years ago, it was customary for devout Christians to ask each other, "What has the Lord given you lately from his Word?" Such a question would inevitably provoke a conversation that increased people's faith. We all need more of that kind of constructive dialogue instead of superficial talk that leads nowhere.

This principle—that our words should strengthen and not diminish faith—can help pastors discern what kind of speech is keeping with the mind of the Spirit in a public meeting. "But everyone who prophesies speaks to men for their *strengthening, encouragement* and comfort" (1 Corinthians 14:3).

Some people have a mistaken view of the gift of prophecy in the New Testament. The stereotypical prophet is a man who condemns everybody, leaving them wounded and bleeding. Scripture offers another picture: "Judas and Silas, *who themselves were prophets,* said much to *encourage* and *strengthen* the brothers" (Acts 15:32).

When sermons, teachings, and exhortations don't build up people's faith, they are not from God, no matter how many Bible verses are quoted. The Lord, better than anyone, knows our need for strong faith and always works toward that end.

When we need to confess our sins and correct our behavior, the Holy Spirit points us to Christ, encouraging us to trust in his grace. I have heard sermons so legalistic and condemnatory that rather than encouraging my faith,

they tempted me to despair that the Lord even loved me!
This pseudo-prophetic nonsense is
not part of the Holy Spirit's min-
istry on earth. If we do not leave   The Lord, better
church with a strengthened faith,   than anyone, knows
then there was no use attending.   our need for strong faith
Without faith, it's impossible to   and always works
please God, and pleasing him is   toward that end.
the aim of all that we do in his
name.

ENCOURAGING PRAYER

When Paul was separated from the believers he cher-
ished, he revealed another avenue for edifying their faith:
"I pray that out of his glorious riches he may strengthen
you with power through his Spirit in your inner being, so
that Christ may dwell in your hearts through faith" (Ephesians 3:16–17).

When Paul could not speak encouragement to the
church, he prayed that the Holy Spirit would carry on the
same work within the believers. He knew Satan's assault
would invariably aim at the faith of the Christian. This
knowledge caused him to do more than teach. He interceded for the believers so that they would be empowered
by the Spirit for greater faith. In essence, intercessory
prayer touches God with one hand while reaching out to
those being prayed for with the other.

The idea of focusing our prayers on strengthening other
Christians "with power through his Spirit" is sadly uncom-
mon today. Instead, many of our church services have

turned into little more than lectures about biblical truth. There is too little personal experience of the things the early church valued, like this kind of prayer. Within seconds of hearing the minister's sermon, many folks are racing to the parking lot. Can we honestly describe our own churches as "houses of prayer"? When was the last time you joined hands with another person right there in church and interceded for each other?

Paul prayed for believers because he knew God answers prayer. He also prayed because "love" always prays for the welfare of the loved one. Encouraging others through prayer is both a privilege and a responsibility. Consider what Samuel said as an old man stepping off the stage as the spiritual leader of Israel: "As for me, far be it from me that I should sin against the LORD by failing to pray for you" (1 Samuel 12:23).

The ministry of intercessory prayer needs to be reemphasized today in the body of Christ. Pastors especially must realize that teaching alone does not fulfill our mandate from God. Too many believers are spiritually asleep or deeply discouraged with little faith. Their prayer life is almost nonexistent. Who will hold them up before the Lord at the throne of grace? Who will keep praying, "that Christ may dwell in your hearts through faith"? We have an abundance of teachers, singers, musicians, worship leaders, and administrators, but a critical shortage of those who will devote themselves to this sacred calling. Not until heaven will we understand the greatness of those who prevailed in prayer for other believers.

ENCOURAGING WORSHIP

There's one more way in which we can all be encouraged in our faith life.

> Let us not give up meeting together, as some are in the habit of doing, but let us encourage one another—and all the more as you see the Day approaching (Hebrews 10:25).

It is a blessing to worship together with other believers. Pastors shouldn't try to keep up attendance by laying guilt-trips on their members to prevent them from staying home from church. Instead, we need to help people realize that corporate prayer is a privilege and that worship can be tremendously edifying. Many times I have walked into the Brooklyn Tabernacle tired and discouraged, only to leave praising the Lord and full of faith. Singing hymns and spiritual songs to the Lord, hearing his precious Word expounded, lifting my voice in prayer with other Christians, loving and being loved—these are the means the Lord uses to strengthen our hearts.

In Paul's day there were people who shunned public worship for one reason or another. Their modern counterparts have little desire to be in God's house with his people. This is a bad thing no matter what the rationalization. I have learned as a pastor that when a believer starts attending church less frequently or only sporadically, it is always a sign of spiritual trouble. I've heard all the rationalizations: "I'm too busy right now" or "We need more time as a family" or "I worship God at home in my kitchen" or the ever-popular "The church is filled with hypocrites." All of these excuses are smoke screens for some kind of spiritual malady.

Worshiping God with other believers is what we're going to be doing for all eternity. Folks who have little appetite to be with other believers have, in fact, little appetite for Christ. To be a healthy part of the body always implies two things: a desire to stay connected, and the humility to admit our need for other believers. If the apostle Paul asked for prayer and longed for fellowship with believers, we should, too. I need the encouragement of brothers and sisters in Christ to help me along my way. What about you?

Don't let disappointment or church politics keep you from experiencing spiritual renewal. Attending church regularly is not a matter of legalism but spiritual logic, especially as we see "the Day" approaching. Soon Jesus will come again, and all the cares of life that bog us down will disappear in a millisecond. What others think, the kind of house we own, the car we drive, and the size of our stock portfolio have no significance in light of eternity. What matters today is our faith in Christ, our growth in grace, the fruit we produce for his glory, and the fulfillment of his will for our lives. Much of our spiritual development happens as we interact with other members of the body of Christ on a regular basis.

When I think of getting priorities straight, I think about an eighty-eight-year-old woman I know named Estelle. She has never had it easy. When Estelle was a child, her father became ill. In 1929, at age fourteen, with the Great Depression just beginning, Estelle moved to New York, hoping to find work to help ease things back home in Pennsylvania. Grateful to have landed a job waiting tables, she sent home three quarters of her salary—$15 a month. That left just $5 to cover her expenses.

By the time she was twenty-one, Estelle married a young man, named Nick, whom she met at church. The first few years of their marriage went well, and both were active in the church, she as a Sunday school teacher and he as secretary-treasurer. Even though the church was very legalistic, Estelle knew that what matters most in life is loving and trusting Jesus.

What she didn't know was that her trust was about to be severely tried, not for a short season, but for the next twenty-three years. The trouble started at one of Nick's office parties. He had attended plenty of them during his career at Westinghouse but had always managed to say a polite no whenever alcoholic beverages were offered. Then one night he gave in, and it only took one drink for him to lose control of himself. In an instant he became an alcoholic. That's when the shouting started and the violence and the tears.

The situation became so bad that even Nick's relatives urged her to leave. "He's going to beat you, if you don't," they warned. "Think of the toll it's taking on the kids."

She knew her children were upset. Her daughter came down with a case of shingles because her nerves were so bad, and her twelve-year-old son began pouring out the bourbon his father had hidden in the basement. She knew Nick wouldn't complain. He wouldn't even admit he drank, so he couldn't possibly object when his bourbon went missing.

As much as she loved her children, Estelle couldn't bring herself to leave her husband. She was too afraid that Nick would end up in the gutter. So she stuck it out. It wasn't long until Nick lost his job at Westinghouse and Estelle went back to work to support the family. For twenty-five years she worked at a large department store in downtown Brooklyn and finally retired in 1981.

During all that time, Estelle never lost faith, never stopped praying that the Lord would reach her husband in a way she couldn't. It was no use quoting Bible verses to him. He knew them all. God would have to find a way to penetrate his heart.

The whole family was praying for Nick. Estelle's youngest son had gone into the ministry and had enlisted people in his church to pray. Finally, when Nick was in his seventies, he stopped drinking. Nothing dramatic happened to change him. But Estelle knew that God had used the prayers of many to convict him of his sin and his need for grace. For the last fifteen years of his life, Nick was sober as a judge.

Today Estelle is the same faith-filled woman she has always been, telling friends and family that "Jesus is sweeter now than ever before." At the age of eighty-eight, her top priority is loving the Lord and serving alongside his people.

As a member of the Brooklyn Tabernacle, Estelle attends at least two of the three worship services every Sunday. She's always early for the Tuesday night prayer service, and she's up again for the Wednesday morning Ladies' Fellowship, where every first-time visitor receives a beautiful potholder, handmade by her. Last year she made and handed out more than four thousand of them!

Many people weaken in their faith as they age, becoming attached to the shallow security of this world or growing cynical from the wear and tear of life. The fiery devotion they once had for the Lord ebbs away. But Estelle is a rebuke to all who let themselves be robbed of their faith and fervency.

A few years ago, Nick passed away. After sixty-four years of married life, Estelle needed fresh grace to deal with the loss. But God is faithful, and she continues to serve him with joy and amazing energy. Instead of bitterness or depression, she has the inner beauty of a heart that leans hard on the Lord. She's probably the prettiest eighty-eight-year-old lady anyone could ever meet. You can take my word for it, because she's my mom.

CHAPTER ELEVEN

BREAK-
THROUGH
Timing

hether it's in business, politics, sports, or standup comedy, experts tell us that timing doesn't mean anything—it means *everything*. Prayer, too, can be a matter of timing. Failure to understand God's timing regarding a matter we are praying about can lead to spiritual disappointment and missed opportunities. Whenever we pray, it's vital to distinguish among four different directives from the Lord. Doing so can give us the breakthrough timing we need in order to do his will. For any given prayer or undertaking in our life, we need to discern whether the Lord is saying one of these four things:

> Never
> Always
> At certain times
> Not now

BREAKTHROUGH *Prayer*

One of my earliest memories of church is of a short chorus I heard the congregation singing. I barely understood the hymn at the time. The words were profound but simple:

> To be like Jesus, to be like Jesus
> All I ask is to be like him,
> All through life's journey, from earth to glory,
> All I ask is to be like him.

The goal of spiritual growth is simply that: To become like Jesus. The Bible declares that from before the creation of the world, God intended us to be "conformed to the likeness of his Son" (Romans 8:29). This is the spiritual yardstick by which we can measure our progress: Are we becoming more like Jesus? Using that measure, we begin to realize that the most Christlike person often is not the one who has memorized the most Scripture or the one most visible in leadership.

Anyone who studies the life of Jesus can't help but be impressed with his unruffled peace and perfect spiritual poise. No matter the situation, the Lord knew what to say and when to say it. He also knew when to be silent. He always did the right thing with perfect timing. He also knew when to withdraw from the clamoring crowds for a time of rest or prayer. Whether he was healing the sick, walking the dusty roads of Judea, or preaching and praying, Jesus' sense of what the moment required was flawless.

This keen understanding of divine imperatives and precise spiritual timing is at the heart of what it means to be mature in Christ. Some things must *never* be done, while others must *always* be observed. *At certain times* a particular action is the only proper course to take; at other times even good things are inappropriate because the Lord is saying *"not now."* Understanding God's imperatives and his timing—his *never, always, at certain times,* and *not now*—can help us avoid painful pitfalls and guide us into his perfect will.

An inability to understand and obey these principles is a mark of spiritual immaturity and carnality. When we fail to believe that God is serious when he says *never,* we suffer the hurtful consequences of our disobedience. The same is true when we respond halfheartedly to an *always* command. But when God responds by saying *"at certain times,"* it can be difficult to know what precisely to do, especially when the decision has no obvious moral quality to it. Just as challenging is the ability to hear God's *"not now"* response, bidding us to cease an otherwise proper course of action.

A most dramatic moment in Old Testament history well illustrates these principles. The Israelites had just left Egypt after the Lord had delivered ten plagues on their enemy. Following the desert road that led to the Red Sea, they had camped at its edge. But Pharaoh, who had let them go with great reluctance, changed his mind once again, pursuing them into the desert with a host of chariots and soldiers.

> As Pharaoh approached, the Israelites looked up, and there were the Egyptians, marching after them. They were terrified and cried out to the LORD. They said to Moses, "Was it because there were no graves in Egypt that you brought us to the desert to die? What have you done to us by bringing us out of Egypt? Didn't we say to you in

Egypt, 'Leave us alone; let us serve the Egyptians'? It would have been better for us to serve the Egyptians than to die in the desert!"

Moses answered the people, "Do not be afraid. Stand firm and you will see the deliverance the LORD will bring you today. The Egyptians you see today you will never see again. The LORD will fight for you; you need only to be still."

Then the LORD said to Moses, "Why are you crying out to me? Tell the Israelites to move on. Raise your staff and stretch out your hand over the sea to divide the water so that the Israelites can go through the sea on dry ground" (Exodus 14:10–16).

GOD'S NEVER WORDS

This was the first spiritual test God's people faced after their emancipation. As Pharaoh's army drew near, they panicked, blaming Moses for delivering them in the first place. It would have been better to have stayed in Egypt as slaves, they reasoned, than to face Pharaoh's chariots with their backs to the sea. Convinced this was the end, they regretted believing in the word of the Lord delivered through Moses. Gone was their memory of how God had powerfully vindicated Moses by raining down plagues of blood, insects, and illness on their Egyptian captors. Gone, too, was their memory of the Passover night, when their children were spared and the Egyptians' children taken. In their moment of crisis, the Israelites couldn't muster an ounce of faith in the God who had already proven his love and faithfulness.

It was in this setting that they heard one of the Lord's most important *never* words, a word that applies to us today. It came through Moses, who boldly declared, "Do not be afraid."

Whether it's the Israelites at the Red Sea or you and I at the beginning of the twenty-first century, fear and timidity are *never* God's will for his people. To be controlled by fear means the death of faith. "Without faith it is impossible to please God" (Hebrews 11:6). It doesn't matter how many chariots pursued the Israelites then or how many terrorist cells plot mayhem today. Fear is never an option for the children of the living God.

When we ignore God's word, "Do not be afraid," we sadden the Spirit of God and forfeit the blessings he intends for us. In fact, fear is far worse than diseases like cancer or AIDS, because they only attack the body while fear assaults the soul. In times of doubt and anxiety, Christians must distinguish themselves by their faith and fearlessness. You may protest when looking at ominous headlines or shaky financial markets and wonder, "How can we not be afraid?" Instead of letting the news control your emotions, read what the Bible declares:

> God is our refuge and strength,
>   an ever-present help in trouble.
> Therefore we will not fear, though the earth give way
>   and the mountains fall into the heart of the sea,
> though its waters roar and foam
>   and the mountains quake with their surging
>   (Psalm 46:1–3).

We should begin every day by reminding ourselves of this *never* word from God. We will not fear, no matter how bad the news or how dire the world may seem, since God is still in control. The psalmist was determined to stay calm and fearless even if the earth itself should give way. Compare his attitude with the jitters we sometimes feel when the government warns that something terrible *might* happen somewhere sometime. To live in fear is as much a disobedience to God as stealing or lying. The same God who said not to covet also declared that we are *never* to fear.

After witnessing the ten plagues, Passover night, the plunder of the Egyptians, and God's pillar of fire guiding them, the Israelites should have trusted the Lord, even with chariots chasing them. God would not forsake them at the Red Sea after doing so much to deliver them, and Pharaoh would not have the last laugh over the Creator of the universe.

> To live in fear is as much a disobedience to God as stealing or lying.

We wonder why the Israelites had so little faith. But how big is our own faith when a crisis occurs? Do we remember that God loves us with an everlasting love; that he sent his only Son to pay the price for our sins; that he made costly provision for our pardon, cleansing, and eternal salvation; that our Savior has gone to prepare a place for us in heaven; that he has sent the Holy Spirit as our comforter and given us precious promises backed by his own great faithfulness? Since God has done all that for us, why should we be afraid even if "the mountains fall into the sea"?

We can't let mood swings challenge God's *never* word to us. We must grow up into our salvation so that bold confidence in our Lord will characterize our daily lives. There is a simple but powerful phrase from Psalm 23 that many of us learned as children: "I will fear no evil." These are not the words of a nursery rhyme, but words from the Bible that can help us live by God's grace regardless of how ominous things seem.

Psalm 34 speaks of a great promise concerning breakthrough prayer. It comes from a time in David's life when King Saul and his army were stalking him. David prayed and received something deeper than deliverance from trouble. "I sought the LORD, and he answered me; he delivered me from all my fears" (Psalm 34:4).

Not only can God protect us from danger, but he can also rescue us from the nagging fear of what *might* happen to us. That kind of anxiety creates spiritual chaos in us, robbing us of joy and peace. As we pray in faith to God, he will give us a nocturnal blessing that will affect both body and soul.

> When you lie down, you will *not be afraid;*
>> when you lie down, your sleep will be sweet.
> *Have no fear* of sudden disaster
>> or of the ruin that overtakes the wicked
>> (Proverbs 3:24–25).

Having faith doesn't mean we can't be honest with God about our struggles with fear. I have battled with strong anxiety before preaching in certain venues even though I knew my fear would hinder the work of the Holy Spirit.

We all have our areas of structural weakness, but so did David, who was especially favored by God.

> When I am afraid,
>> I will trust in you.
> In God, whose word I praise,
>> in God I trust; I will not be afraid.
>> What can mortal man do to me? (Psalm 56:3–4).

David doesn't say, "I am never attacked by fear," but rather "when I am afraid, I will trust in you. . . . I will not be afraid." We are assaulted by fears of every kind, but we needn't let them find a resting place in our hearts. Break through into a new confidence in God that dethrones fear and keeps it from ruling our lives. As we walk by faith and not by sight, we can rest in the words of Jesus that have comforted so many before us: "Don't be afraid; just believe" (Mark 5:36).

GOD'S ALWAYS WORDS

While making it clear that we must never be afraid, Moses conveyed another of God's imperatives to the people: "Stand firm and you will see the deliverance [of] the LORD" (Exodus 14:13). God's people must *always stand firm in faith* no matter what happens around them. The basic truth of salvation is that "the righteous will live by faith" (Galatians 3:11). This same faith should characterize our daily life in Christ. Faith brings stability in times of uncertainty while unbelief causes vacillation. The apostle Paul wrote words to the believers in Corinth that still apply to us today: "Be on your guard; stand firm in the faith; be men of courage; be strong" (1 Corinthians 16:13).

That almost sounds like a locker-room pep talk before a big football game. In fact, it is God's directive for each day of our lives: *Always* walk by faith in the Lord.

Not sometimes or most times, but always have faith and be courageous in God. Christians whose faith gets wobbly in times of stress and difficulty must remember, "It is *by faith* you stand firm" (2 Corinthians 1:24). "Trying harder" to do the right thing is not what's needed. Instead, we must have faith in what God can and will do for us.

When the Israelites were pinned between the Red Sea and Pharaoh's army, God said, "Stand firm in faith." Pharaoh's chariots came thundering down on a people who had absolutely no military experience, yet God said, "Trust me to handle this."

This *always* word from God was written for our instruction and encouragement today as we face a post-9/11 world filled with nuclear and biological terror. We must stand firm, be strong in the Lord, and face the future with courage.

> "Trying harder" to do the right thing is not what's needed. Instead, we must have faith in what God can and will do for us.

If you doubt the importance of standing firm in faith, consider the alternative: "If you do not stand firm in your faith, you will not stand at all" (Isaiah 7:9). If your trust in God falters, you are flirting with disaster. These are not melodramatic words, but a warning rooted in Scripture.

So do not throw away your confidence; it will be richly rewarded. You need to persevere so that when you have done the will of God, you will receive what he has promised. For in just a little while,

"He who is coming will come and will not delay.
   But my righteous one will live by faith.
And if he shrinks back,
   I will not be pleased with him."

But we are not of those who shrink back and are destroyed, but of those who believe and are saved (Hebrews 10:35–39).

No matter what or who threatens us, we must seek the face of God and look to him in faith. Don't lose your confidence when others who once clung to Christ fall away. Remember the word of caution from the Lord: If we shrink back in unbelief, God will not be pleased with us.

AT CERTAIN TIMES

Backed up against the sea with the enemy pursuing, Moses gave an unusual command: "The LORD will fight for you; *you need only to be still*." That day, God would destroy the Egyptian army without one Israelite striking a blow. His people had to let him do the work while quietly observing his hand of power.

The way God guided his people that day doesn't mean he will act that way in every situation. It doesn't automatically follow that we should always sit quietly, letting God do all the work. This was God's word for a particular moment, one that applies *at certain times.*

Unfortunately, some Christians have tried to make a complete theology out of this and similar passages, emphasizing that God will always do the fighting for us. According to them, believers are merely to watch passively for the salvation of the Lord, no matter the circumstances. Some people emphasize another story from the Bible in which the Israelites sang and worshiped as God overcame their enemies. They use it to try to prove that praising God is the secret to success in *every* situation. These mistaken interpretations have given birth to quietist groups, who concentrate solely on "waiting," as well as to "praise and worship" churches that prescribe almost nothing but making a joyful noise to the Lord.

> When it comes to being led by the Lord, there are no simple formulas that apply to every situation.

When it comes to being led by the Lord, there are no simple formulas that apply to every situation. We need to learn to follow God's leading day by day. When Moses directed the Israelites to stand still and observe the power of God, he was not laying down a principle to be obeyed in all situations. In fact, in the centuries that followed, it was the armies of Israel, commanded by people like Joshua, David, and Joab, that God used to overcome the enemies who threatened his people.

If we are going to break through into new power in prayer and service to others, we must make a deeper acquaintance with the Holy Spirit of God. In the same way that God instructed Moses to direct the people to stand still, the Spirit of God is able to lead us in every new situation we face. Such cases do not call for simple commands like "do not lie" or "do not steal," but subtler, *at-certain-times* directions that only the Spirit can impart.

It is a shame that evangelical seminaries and churches often downplay the importance of the Holy Spirit. According to them, the Spirit is the author of Scripture and the one who convicts the world of sin. But much more is attributed to the Holy Spirit in the Bible he inspired. Without being Spirit-led, we cannot possibly live victoriously for Christ. We are not smart enough to know on our own what the will of God is in each situation we encounter. Has the Holy Spirit departed this earth so we can no longer experience his guidance as did the early church?

If the apostles of the early church returned to earth today, they would be shocked by our cavalier dismissal of the idea of being led by the Spirit. While many warn of fanaticism and mystical excesses, others contend that we don't need God's supernatural direction anymore because we have the canon of Scripture. But how would the moral precepts of all sixty-six books of the Bible have helped Paul to know God's will at a particular moment of his missionary journeys?

> Paul and his companions traveled throughout the region of Phrygia and Galatia, *having been kept by the Holy Spirit* from preaching the word in the province of Asia. When they came to the border of Mysia, they tried to enter Bithynia, but *the Spirit of Jesus would not allow them to* (Acts 16:6–7).

The apostle and his companions weren't hoping to enter Asia (modern Turkey) in order to sell magazine subscriptions. They wanted to spread the gospel *at a certain point in time* in a certain place. But the Lord had other plans. When they attempted to make their way into Bithynia, "the Spirit of Jesus would not allow them to." The book of Acts doesn't describe how the Spirit made his will known, but it does make it clear that God was the one who altered their plans. Paul and his companions were not left confused and idle for long, because whenever people are willing to be led, the Lord is faithful to reveal what they should do at any particular moment.

> During the night Paul had a vision of a man of Macedonia standing and begging him, "Come over to Macedonia and help us." After Paul had seen the vision, we got ready at once to leave for Macedonia, concluding that *God had called us* to preach the gospel to them (Acts 16:9–10).

Breakthrough timing is all about knowing the exact will of God at a given moment. The Lord doesn't expect us to try to understand his plan for our lives merely by relying on our limited intelligence. He has sent the Holy Spirit to guide our steps in the paths he has marked out for us. We are not talking about resolving moral questions, but about making important decisions at life's crossroads.

> Whenever people are willing to be led, the Lord is faithful to reveal what they should do at any particular moment.

In the case of the Israelites, each new battle meant discovering what God's strategy for them might be. The Lord's direction for them at the Red Sea was merely his plan for victory at that particular time; the battle for Jericho would yield a different military strategy. It is the same for us today. God the Holy Spirit will show us the best path to follow if we are willing to be led by him.

We need to ask the Lord to guide us as we try to raise our children in the Lord, because each one is different. Each child offers a unique challenge. The same goes for changing jobs, relocating, or finding a new church. The God who directed the Israelites for forty years in the wilderness is still able to lead his children. Sadly, too few of us make these kinds of decisions a matter of earnest prayer and open our hearts to the Spirit's leading. Rather than longing for communion with the living God, most pastors are searching frantically for techniques that "work." But they have forgotten that nothing produces *spiritual* results like being led by the Spirit.

WHEN GOD SAYS NOT NOW

The last part of our Bible story is the most unusual of all. Rarely do we read of God telling someone to stop praying, but that is exactly what happened.

> Then the LORD said to Moses, "*Why are you crying out to me?* Tell the Israelites to move on. Raise your staff and stretch out your hand over the sea to divide the water so that the Israelites can go through the sea on dry ground" (Exodus 14:15–16).

Prayer is precious to the Lord, a fact that makes this passage all the more striking. Moses was doing a noble thing, but God directed him to stop. He wanted Moses to do something better—to act in faith so that God could deliver his people from Pharaoh's army. Sometimes even the best of activities must come to a halt at the command of God so a critical deed can be accomplished.

A man I know was almost murdered forty years ago on a rooftop in the Bronx. This man was so strung out on heroin that he couldn't think of anything but his next fix. Desperate for more drugs, George did one of the stupidest things an addict can do: He stole heroin from a drug dealer. When the enraged dealer, a guy named "Crazy Joe," and his sidekick caught up with him in an abandoned building,

> Sometimes even the best of activities must come to a halt at the command of God so a critical deed can be accomplished.

threatening to cut him into a thousand pieces, George didn't beg for his life but merely said, "Do what you have to do—just let me get high."

Realizing he was about to witness a murder, Crazy Joe's accomplice argued that George's life wasn't worth taking, since he was nothing but a dirty drug addict. Amazingly, the irate drug dealer softened and let George go. What had seemed like the certain end of his life turned into one more chance to receive help. George had had other opportunities. He was once released from the Rikers Island prison to attend a drug program. Another time, he overdosed on heroin and ended up in the hospital, surrounded by police. That time he was so freaked out that he jumped out of a window to get away.

George's brush with death with Crazy Joe was the experience that finally got the message through his head. Soon after, he turned away from a life of drug abuse and entered a Christian rehab program, where he learned to live victoriously through faith in God.

The change was remarkable. The former addict became walking proof of the truth found in 2 Corinthians 5:17: "The old has gone, the new has come!"

After completing the program, George served on staff for a year and then attended Bible school. Two weeks after graduating, George married his school sweetheart and settled down to work at the Detention Center run by the Commonwealth of Massachusetts. His clients, who were eight-to-fifteen-year-old boys, were mostly runaways and thieves, with a handful of murderers thrown in. But as far as George was concerned, this was a dream assignment. He felt the Lord calling him to help hurting people, just as he had been helped in his time of despair.

But no matter how hard he prayed and worked, George made little progress with the kids. The program seemed a complete failure. It didn't help that some of his coworkers kept getting high on drugs themselves, spending more time at meetings, lunch appointments, and after-hours office parties than with the young people they were supposed to help.

Things got worse before they got better. George's next job was as the outside program director at Walpole Prison. Oddly, the prisoners themselves ran the therapeutic program at the prison. George didn't mind interviewing with a small committee who would decide whether to hire him. But he did think it was strange that the committee was composed entirely of convicted murderers.

Still, George kept praying for direction, determined to break through the bureaucratic inertia and ineffectiveness of the government programs for which he worked. His efforts met with only disillusionment and disappointment. Why wasn't God answering his prayers for help?

George's last assignment was as an aftercare worker at the Boston City Methadone Clinic. There was only one problem: There was no aftercare. George worked for several months without even one client because addicts simply came to the clinic to secure their supply of methadone, a synthetic addictive drug used to replace heroin. When he finally did get a client, it was someone who was new to the program and needed help filling out government forms. George spent six hours helping him fill out the required stack of paperwork. That was it.

George had gone into social services to help people, but he felt as if he wasn't making a difference. Had he mistaken God's call on his life, missed some sign from heaven that would have directed his steps another way? Though George didn't realize it at the time, his fervent prayers had been answered, but with a *not now* word from God. Everything that had happened in George's life was preparation for what he would be doing in the future.

God was about to act. He began by placing a desire in George's wife's heart that soon caught fire in his heart as well.

George Rosado, the former junkie, had married Grace, the pastor's daughter. Together they established New Life, a ministry that has been helping hundreds of hurting women in New England and elsewhere for more than twenty-five years.

If you happened to be in New Hampshire and dropped by to see George and Grace, you would see that the ministry is located in a spacious house. Every morning the women who live there gather for a Bible study, and among them sits Farah, the young woman from Haiti whose life had once seemed so hopeless. Three lives that God touched with his grace have come together in a marvelous way.

There are more wonderful things to come that we can't even imagine. Beautiful, life-changing breakthroughs are what God is all about.

CHAPTER TWELVE

BREAK-
THROUGH
Joy

uch of the political debate in the United States revolves not only around the stock market or threats of terrorism, but also the soaring costs of health care. Although the country is fortunate to have treatments and prescription drugs for almost every malady, many people simply cannot afford them. The nightly news is filled with stories about health management organizations (HMOs), drug company profits, doctor's fees, and the plight of senior citizens living on fixed incomes.

We want access to the best medical treatment possible throughout the course of our lives. As Christians we thank God for the blessings of modern medicine that relieve so much human suffering. But no matter how rich we are, no matter what kind of health plan we have, there are still

No matter how rich we are, no matter what kind of health plan we have, there are still some antibiotics we can obtain only from God's pharmacy.

some antibiotics we can obtain only from God's pharmacy.

Our loving Creator fashioned us in his likeness and is deeply concerned for our welfare. In addition to having a physical body and a soul, each of us is also a *spiritual* being. This is why the apostle Paul prayed, "May your *whole spirit, soul and body* be kept blameless at the coming of our Lord Jesus Christ" (1 Thessalonians 5:23). It is this spiritual dimension that makes us unique and separates humankind from the rest of creation.

THE KEYS TO SPIRITUAL HEALTH

Most of the time we are more preoccupied with our bodies than our spirits. But my spirit, the essential "Jim Cymbala," and its state of being can have a strong affect on the rest of me. I may be taking daily doses of barley green, flaxseed, and fish oil. I may be popping vitamins and working out. I may be consuming vast amounts of fruits and vegetables. Yet I may have poor *spiritual* health. Just as there are natural laws governing physical well-being, so there are also certain keys to robust *spiritual* health. These keys are presented in Scripture.

Let's visit God's pharmacy and learn from the Word of God about a key building block of vigorous spiritual health: "A joyful heart is good medicine, but a broken spirit dries up the bones" (Proverbs 17:22 NASB).

The Bible focuses on the state of the "heart," which here stands for the human spirit, as the critical factor. In this case it is a *joy-filled, cheerful* inner being that brings a widespread soundness to the whole person. A crushed spirit has the opposite affect. Although joy is vital to our well-being, we rarely pray for it. When is the last time you heard someone pray, "Lord, fill me with the joy you promised me"? This is what I call one of the forgotten prayers of the Bible. It's something God wants to give us, but we have to ask for it. Believing, praying Christians should be filled with the joy of the Lord.

The New King James Version, which comes closer to the meaning of the Hebrew text, renders the verse, "A merry heart does good, like medicine." Literally, it could read, "A merry heart works a good healing, brings good improvement, and powerfully advances the recovery." The root of the Hebrew word denotes the healing of a wound even to the removal of a scar. The "medicine" that brings such deep healing is a heart filled with the joy of the Lord. In stark contrast, a broken or crushed spirit dries up the bones. Joy is vital to our spiritual well-being.

ABC World News Tonight recently told a story that seems to bear out this point. A lab technician from Rochester, Minnesota, fell and shattered her wrist while walking to work one day. The damage was so bad that she said it looked as though she had been thrown through a car windshield. How had a woman who took great pains to maintain her health by exercising regularly, eating well, and taking vitamin and mineral supplements sustained such an injury?

Even her doctors were surprised by the amount of damage she had suffered. "Usually a woman that age can sustain a fall and put their wrist out and catch themselves and not have any problem," said her physician, Dr. Lorraine Fitzpatrick of the Mayo Clinic. "But she had this very bad fracture."[1]

While operating to repair the damage, doctors discovered the problem. This forty-six-year-old woman had unusually brittle bones. The diagnosis was advanced osteoporosis. Dr. Fitzpatrick commented that her patient had the bones of a woman fifteen-to-twenty years older. Doctors believe the problem may have stemmed from a bout of depression the woman had suffered years earlier. Apparently there is significant evidence showing that depression can lead to bone density loss in both men and women.

A recent medical study offered X-ray evidence of the bone density loss in women who suffered even mild depression compared with those who never suffered depression. The study revealed that when depression lifted, new pockets of calcium would amazingly form and strengthen the weakened bones. Ironically, in that verse from Proverbs, Solomon spoke through the Holy Spirit concerning this more than three thousand years ago.

Think about the spiritual maladies that affect us. Consider, too, the negative influence these maladies have on our families and our ability to witness for Christ. Many people plod through their days with a sour, irritable spirit that is corrosive to themselves and others. I once counseled a pastor whose spirit was so bitter that even his wife couldn't bear his sermons. His messages were not doctrinally wrong, but he drove everyone away with the attitude of his heart.

We can't run the race of life while weighed down by a bitter spirit. I am saddened when I think of some single adults whose sour, irritable ways may prevent them from finding the companion they long for. Others have hearts loaded down by care and anxiety. Constant worry robs many people of the spiritual resources God gladly provides. Eventually anxiety crushes us under its weight. This is not pop psychology, but the truth of God's Word: "An anxious heart weighs a man down" (Proverbs 12:25).

The word for "anxious" is translated in the King James Version as "heaviness," vividly depicting the burdensome effect worry has on us. Anxiety has taken a terrible toll on many people in the body of Christ. Instead of walking by faith, we are prone to walk by worry. Our spirits trudge wearily through life instead of soaring like an eagle, as God promised they would. We are spiritually grounded by anxiety, which only worsens our situation.

> Many people plod through their days with a sour, irritable spirit that is corrosive to themselves and others.

Also, there is the "crushed spirit" of deep sorrow. The apostle Paul cautioned the believers at Corinth to comfort an erring brother who had been reprimanded by the church. This brother had repented of his sin, and Paul was concerned that he might now be "overwhelmed by excessive sorrow" (2 Corinthians 2:7). Another time, Paul expressed gratitude that God had kept an ailing associate minister from dying, sparing the apostle "sorrow upon sorrow" (Philippians 2:27). Paul knew the numbing and disabling effect of a heart swamped by sorrow.

A SPIRITUAL CURE

The cure God offers for these maladies is simply the *joy of the Lord*. Real joy is not mere "happiness," a feeling that fluctuates with our circumstances. Rather, it is a deep, inner delight in God that only the Holy Spirit can produce. This divine joy is more than medicine. It is our strength! "Do not grieve, for the joy of the LORD is your strength" (Nehemiah 8:10).

This is the strength we need to engage in spiritual warfare. Otherwise, Satan, who has many cunning strategies, will try to get us to begin our days with a joyless attitude. Thus weakened, we make easy targets for even heavier satanic artillery aimed at destroying our faith.

George Mueller, a spiritual giant and man of faith of the nineteenth century, asserted that he couldn't safely start a new day without first being "happy in God." Mueller was a man who trusted God to feed thousands of orphans in his care over the course of several decades. He found this happiness by starting every day with prayer and meditation on Scripture. He learned valuable secrets about faith in God, one of which concerns the fortifying element of joy: "May the God of hope fill you with *all joy* and peace as you *trust in him*" (Romans 15:13).

If we are going to walk victoriously by faith, we must maintain a daily spirit of joy in the Lord. Trust and joylessness cannot coexist for very long. The positive effects of joy reach to the very perimeter of our being: "A happy heart makes the face cheerful" (Proverbs 15:13).

> Glum and despondent believers should be sued for false advertising— Jesus Christ is far greater than they're letting on.

Some people who attend church and sing hymns about God's love look as if they were baptized in lemon juice. This fact is sadder than it is funny. Christians should be the happiest people on earth, with smiles that proclaim God's goodness. Glum and despondent believers should be sued for false advertising—Jesus Christ is far greater than they're letting on.

I will never forget a woman in the church I attended as a kid who always wore a black dress, black shoes, a black coat, and black stockings (and those stockings weren't even "in" yet). She never sat with anyone, never talked to anyone, and never smiled. I certainly couldn't imagine her ever laughing. Once I asked an adult why the "lady in black" seemed so downcast. His answer puzzled me. He said she looked that way because she walked with God and lived a holy life. If that were true, I wondered what she would look like if she backslid.

Many people throughout church history have made the very same mistake about what holiness looks like. Contrary to what I was told as a youngster, I believe that those who live closest to God are the most joyful people on the planet. Although my own experience in church may have been different from yours, we all need this reminder: "For the kingdom of God is not a matter of eating and drinking, but of righteousness, peace and joy in the Holy Spirit" (Romans 14:17).

We have all heard sermons exalting the righteousness of Christ and the peace of God. The kingdom of God also has to do with this gift of joy, a gift he bestows on everyone who belongs to him. Joy, in fact, is an important piece of biblical evidence showing that a person has truly turned to Christ for salvation:

> The disciples were filled with joy and with the Holy Spirit (Acts 13:52).

> You welcomed the message with the joy given by the Holy Spirit. And so you became a model to all the believers in Macedonia and Achaia (1 Thessalonians 1:6–7).

Let's not miss what God is saying here. If we are not living with joy, we have to ask ourselves why. With God:

- All our sins have been completely erased through the blood of Jesus.
- There is no record of even one transgression against us before a holy God.
- Our names have been written in the Lamb's book of life.
- Christ has gone to prepare a place for us in heaven, where we will spend eternity with him—which means, for instance, that the worst a terrorist can do is transfer us into our Father's arms.
- The Lord has promised never to leave or forsake us while we live here on earth.
- God has given the Holy Spirit as our Comforter and his Word to guide us into his arms.
- God has pledged to supply our needs and hear us when we pray.

With all this in our favor, how can we trudge through life with a gloomy spirit? What else can our Savior do to make us rejoice in him? If we can't be happy, who can be?

You may think this is not a realistic theological position. With all the troubles and heartaches life brings, it's difficult to imagine leading a life full of such joy. But it's possible because God supernaturally supplies his joy to us through the Holy Spirit. It is "the joy of the Lord," not some hyped-up happiness, that sustains us despite the trials we may pass through. This is why the apostle declares: "But the fruit of the Spirit is love, *joy* ..." (Galatians 5:22).

It would be absurd to imagine that the love we are to show one another originates with us. After all, Jesus said, "As I have loved you, so you must love one another" (John 13:34). It must be the Spirit working in me that produces a Jesus kind of love. The same is true for joy. Our moods vacillate like the stock market, but the Spirit's joy is quite another matter. Paul boldly testified, "In all our troubles my joy knows no bounds" (2 Corinthians 7:4). He characterized himself as "sorrowful, yet always rejoicing" (2 Corinthians 6:10). This godly servant of Christ experienced fierce persecution and understood real sorrow. Yet underneath it all was a mighty river of joy from God. Some of us fret for days over trivial things, yet Paul sang for joy at midnight in a prison. He would ask the same question of us that he did of the Christians in Galatia, "What has happened to all your joy?" (Galatians 4:15).

We don't have to live with heavy, cheerless hearts. When we are full of God's joy, every ordinary day becomes a happy celebration of his goodness. If that seems an exaggeration, listen to this: "All the days of the oppressed are wretched, but the *cheerful heart has a continual feast*" (Proverbs 15:15).

Joy-filled believers don't require endless holidays or nonstop entertainment to make them merry. The world, with all its shallow entertainments, can't satisfy our spiritual need for God. The Lord provides a perpetual banquet through his own presence, just as the Scriptures indicate: "Though you have not seen him, you love him; and even though you do not see him now, you believe in him and are filled with an *inexpressible and glorious joy*" (1 Peter 1:8).

We desperately need a spiritual breakthrough so we can experience triumphant joy rather than the gloom and lifelessness we often see in our churches. Only then will Scripture's word-picture of the early church be true of us: "They broke bread in their homes and ate together with glad and sincere hearts" (Acts 2:46). A fresh visit from the Holy Spirit can produce a new stream of joy from the Lord.

Lynette Mohammed has learned to find joy in the midst of life's trials. If you had asked Lynette two years ago who her best friend was, she wouldn't have skipped a beat. It was Boyie, her husband of twenty-four years. The two had met as youngsters in Trinidad, West Indies, and Boyie had been her first and only boyfriend. After they married, the two did everything together. They were the epitome of a couple in love with Jesus and each other.

Boyie and Lynette lived in Brooklyn with their two children, who were in their early twenties. Every day, Boyie went off to work in downtown Manhattan. The view of the city was breathtaking from the ninety-third floor of

Tower One of the World Trade Center, where he worked. He was there on September 11, 2001, when both towers collapsed from a terrorist attack.

Both Boyie and Lynette were dedicated followers of Christ and members of the Brooklyn Tabernacle. I spoke to Lynette two days after the attack, searching for the right words with which to comfort her. Although Mayor Rudolf Giuliani still held out hope for possible survivors, things looked pretty grim. Lynette had already accepted the fact that her husband would never come home again. She had lost her best friend.

One Sunday Lynette and her daughter stood on the platform together as the entire Brooklyn Tabernacle called on "the God of all comfort" to help our sister and give her consolation. I can still see her with hands lifted and tears running down her cheeks.

Lynette struggled most at night when she was alone in her bedroom. Without Boyie, the house seemed strange, and it was filled with painful reminders. I spoke almost daily with Lynette, and one day I called to find out how she was doing.

"Pastor, thanks for calling," she replied. "The Lord has been so good to me." Her voice and spirit seemed strong and vibrant.

"The other night the most wonderful thing happened. I couldn't sleep, so I went into the living room to spend time with the Lord. I sat in his presence and told him how hard it was to carry on without my husband. Oh Pastor, his Spirit came to me as I was sitting there, and he flooded me with not only peace, but his joy also. I began singing and worshiping God there in my living room as if I was in a sanctuary filled with other Christians. Oh Pastor, God has been so good to me!"

I was stunned. I was the one who had called to encourage Lynette, and here she was, lifting my spirits. The fullness of her joy flooded over into my life, and I praised God for his faithfulness and tender care. Lynette needed all that comfort and more in the months that followed.

> I was the one who had called to encourage Lynette, and here she was, lifting my spirits.

Just as she was healing from the tragic loss of 9/11, Lynette was contacted by the city with news that her husband's "body" had been found. This news took Lynette back to a painful time, but she carried on with stamina and a cheerful heart.

To make matters worse, Lynette's grown son had been troubled by deep emotional problems for several years. Though I knew the family was gravely concerned for him, no one anticipated that he would commit suicide only months after his father's tragic death. Once again Lynette's heart was shattered. But the same God who comforted her after the loss of her husband consoled her again at the loss of her son.

If you visit the Brooklyn Tabernacle, you will find Lynette serving in the hospitality ministry. She is one of the folks who makes the long Sunday schedule easier on the pastoral staff, the musicians, and any special guests present. Though she has an attractive, youthful appearance, her smile is what stands out. Whether serving food or greeting guests, she fulfills, through supernatural grace, the wise word spoken by Moses long ago: "You are to rejoice before the LORD your God in everything you put your hand to" (Deuteronomy 12:18).

We need to follow Lynette's example so that we, too, follow the counsel of Scripture. It is not enough to rejoice once a week in church or when our circumstances seem rosy. Like Lynette, we must rejoice in the Lord in everything we put our hands to.

Living in the joy of the Lord can serve as a great preventive against unhealthy words and actions. If we can't honestly "rejoice before the Lord" while listening, saying, or doing something, we shouldn't engage in those activities, because they can't possibly be good for our souls.

Today is the first day of all the days you have left to live. That makes it the perfect—and only—time to begin. Difficult and painful times may be facing you, but God's joy is greater! It was for you and me that God had the prophet testify:

> Though the fig tree does not bud
>   and there are no grapes on the vines,
> though the olive crop fails
>   and the fields produce no food,
> though there are no sheep in the pen
>   and no cattle in the stalls,
> yet I will rejoice in the LORD,
>   I will be joyful in God my Savior (Habakkuk 3:17–18).

CHAPTER THIRTEEN

BEYOND
Breakthrough

*W*hat would you ask for if you were absolutely certain God would give you anything you wanted? Long life? Riches? A great marriage? Healthy children? A successful career? A fruitful ministry? The one man in the Bible who was given exactly this promise asked for something quite surprising. His name was Solomon, and his story illustrates the unexpected and unimaginable results that can occur when our prayers touch the heart of God in a special way.

Solomon was King David's son and heir. Let's look at the setting for his momentous prayer and God's incredible response:

> The king went to Gibeon to offer sacrifices, for that was the most important high place, and Solomon offered a thousand burnt offerings on that altar. At Gibeon the LORD appeared to Solomon during the night in a dream,

and God said, "Ask for whatever you want me to give you" (1 Kings 3:4–5).

In response to the young king's extravagant and expensive sacrifices—a thousand burnt offerings—the Lord responded to Solomon's display of love with an incredible offer: "Ask for whatever you want me to give you"! God's offer seems especially gracious in light of the fact that Solomon had already made several mistakes since ascending to the throne of his father David. First, he made an alliance with Pharaoh, king of Egypt. Then he made matters worse by marrying Pharaoh's daughter to cement the alliance. Both actions were prohibited by the law of God. Further, we are told that although Solomon loved the Lord, he permitted acts of worship to be carried out improperly:

> Solomon showed his love for the LORD by walking according to the statutes of his father David, *except* that he offered sacrifices and burned incense on the high places (1 Kings 3:3).

The "high places" mentioned in this passage were associated with the idolatrous worship traditions of the local Canaanite tribes. God had commanded Moses to warn the people not to mix pagan elements with their own worship. Even so, Israel eventually incorporated pagan rites and "sacred places" into their own religious practices. In this case, instead of offering sacrifices properly at the tabernacle, Solomon expressed his devotion to the God of Israel at Gibeon, which was the most important high place.

You might wonder why God didn't depose Solomon, forcing him off the throne because of his spiritual weakness. Or why didn't he send fire from heaven to obliterate the pagan shrine at Gibeon? Instead, he looked past Solomon's frailties and mixed-up theology and responded to his worship with a carte blanche offer to fulfill his next prayer, whatever it might be.

Aren't you glad that God is full of mercy and compassion? Though many turn Christianity into a legalistic tit-for-tat theology, isn't it true that God has shown amazing patience with all of us? Haven't some of his choicest blessings come at times when we were not doing splendidly in our walk with him? Hasn't his gracious attitude toward our shortcomings been what has melted our hearts and drawn us close to him? I don't know about anyone else, but as I look back over my own life, all I see is "goodness and mercy" written in large letters over my feeble efforts to serve Christ.

> Though Solomon was flawed, he also loved the Lord, and it was this love that God focused on.

Yet this is not to excuse sin or justify disobedience. Rather, it is to portray the setting for one of the most amazing prayers ever prayed. Though Solomon was flawed, he also loved the Lord, and it was this love that God focused on. That's why I am profoundly thankful for this portion of Scripture. My best sermons and prayers are never what they should or could be, yet God keeps on working with me all the same. Thank God for his long-suffering love that delights in mercy!

FOUR ELEMENTS OF PRAYER

King Solomon's powerful petition has four key elements that can instruct our own prayers:

1. *Solomon approached God first with thanks and praise.*

> "Now, O LORD my God, *you have made your servant king* in place of my father David" (1 Kings 3:7a).

Solomon began by praising and thanking God for placing him on the throne. He acknowledged that he had come to his position, not by an accident of history nor because of superior qualifications, but because of God's gracious choice. How surprising that Solomon, the son of David and Bathsheba, would have become king at all!

Bathsheba, you will remember, was the woman David seduced while her husband was away at war. When she became pregnant with his child, David arranged for her husband to be murdered in battle in order to cover up the sin. Solomon would have known that he should have had little hope of inheriting his father's throne. In fact, his mother's name would only remind people of King David's moral failure. But God allowed Solomon to become king and Bathsheba's name to go down in history. No wonder God, who is so different from us, is called the "father of mercies"!

Like Solomon we should approach God with praise on our lips. Everything we are and everything we have comes from him. As Scripture tells us, "Every good and perfect gift is from above, coming down from the Father of the heavenly lights" (James 1:17). Let us not approach the throne of grace with a complaining spirit, but rather by counting our blessings and thanking God for each of them.

2. Solomon prayed with great humility.

"But I am only a little child and do not know how to carry out my duties" (v. 7b).

Instead of boasting about his superior education or his being trained by Israel's finest leaders, Solomon acknowledged that he was unfit for such an important position unless God equipped him. Amazingly, the king who would become known as the wisest man in history compared himself to a little child. Solomon's belief in his natural inability is exactly what qualified him to receive supernatural help. His humble spirit helped to unlock the treasury of heaven.

The same holds true for us. If we humble ourselves before God, he will certainly lift us up. But if we rely on our own abilities, connections, or position, we will receive little help from God.

3. Solomon defined himself as God's servant, ready to do his will.

"Your *servant* is here among the people you have chosen, a great people, too numerous to count or number" (v. 8).

Three times in his brief prayer Solomon referred to himself, not as the king, but as God's *servant*. No wonder he received such an incredible answer to prayer! A servant's task is simple—to follow orders. Solomon had no thought of "using" God but instead displayed a fervent desire to be used *by* him. This was Solomon's attitude as he prepared to respond to God's invitation to ask for whatever he wanted.

4. *Solomon asked for a blessing that would bless God's people.*

"So give your servant a discerning heart to govern your people and to distinguish between right and wrong. For who is able to govern this great people of yours?" (v. 9).

This final portion of Solomon's prayer was the real key to God's overwhelming response. Rather than asking selfishly for himself, Solomon called on the Lord for help so *he might serve God's people effectively*. He asked for a wise and discerning heart so that he might govern fairly and lead Israel with wisdom. When God heard his request for a blessing that would *make him a blessing to others,* he answered with such liberality that Solomon became the richest and most glorious king of his time.

Solomon's petition highlights an often overlooked facet of prayer. The Lord took notice that he didn't ask for himself but rather was concerned for the welfare of God's own people. By contrast, almost all of our prayers have to do only with *us*—what *we* lack, the challenges *we* face, the needs of *our* family.

The LORD was pleased that Solomon had asked for this. So God said to him, "Since you have asked for this and not for long life or wealth for yourself, nor have asked for the death of your enemies but for discernment in administering justice, I will do what you have asked. I will give you a wise and discerning heart, so that there will never have been anyone like you, nor will there ever be. Moreover, I will give you what you have not asked for—both riches and honor—so that in your lifetime you will have no equal among kings" (vv. 10–13).

What an outpouring of God's favor on young Solomon! Because he asked unselfishly, God blessed him far beyond what he asked. The same principle still applies. When we learn to pray more for God's people than for ourselves, we will find a liberality of response beyond what we can ask or imagine. Remember that God intends not only to supply our needs through prayer but to make us channels of his blessings so that we can bless others in his name.

> God intends to make us channels of his blessings so that we can bless others in his name.

A SURPRISE BLESSING

As I was putting the finishing touches on this book, a remarkable set of circumstances unfolded in the life of the church. I wondered about God's timing. It seemed as though he might be making a point, wanting me to encourage you with an up-to-the-minute report about his desire to bless his people with surprising answers to their prayers.

During a recent Sunday afternoon service at the Brooklyn Tabernacle, a children's choir from Uganda sang and presented the gospel. The children were orphans whose parents had died from the AIDS epidemic ravaging Africa. Prior to the meeting, one of the leaders asked if he could show a ten-minute video about their ministry to orphans. Always careful about subjecting the congregation to yet another request for money, I was hesitant, unsure whether the video would be appropriate in the worship service. But after the children sang and shared their love for Jesus, I felt led to show the video at the close of the service. It was a powerful story of a ministry reaching out to some of the most vulnerable children on earth.

As we watched this moving testimony on screen, I prayed that God would show me how to lead the service. Should the children continue singing? Should I close the service with an invitation for people to receive Christ? As I sought the Lord, I felt directed to take a special offering to help the ministry in Uganda.

But the church was under intense financial pressure at the time. Just that week I learned we didn't have the money to complete the last phase of a multimillion dollar construction project. If any church needed every dollar it could put its hands on, we were it. And here we were in the inner city, I reasoned, with our own critical needs, doing our best to help hurting people around us. Anyway, we had just taken our own general collection fifty minutes earlier. How could we raise up another offering so soon after for this ministry in Africa?

These thoughts flitted through my mind for a few seconds, but the voice in my heart quickly overpowered them: "You know what you should do. Give a generous offering and help these people. Just bless them and trust me to look after you and your needs." I felt prompted to start the giving with the $100 bill that happened to be in my billfold. When the video ended, I walked out on the platform and told the audience what I felt the Lord wanted us to do. There was a great sense of confirmation among everyone, and an offering was taken as the children from Uganda sang a few more songs. The meeting closed soon afterward, and I went home convinced that I had obeyed the Lord.

Two days later, I ran into our financial administrator, who asked if I knew the amount of that second offering we took on Sunday. She happily told me that more than $23,000 had come in for the ministry. What amazing generosity by mostly poor people for a wonderful ministry doing God's work in Africa! I went into my office overjoyed that I had done what God wanted me to do.

About two hours later I received an unexpected call from a woman in another part of the country. She explained that she had been reading my book *Fresh Wind, Fresh Fire* and wanted to inquire about the work we were doing for the Lord in downtown Brooklyn. She said she had recently come into an inheritance and wanted to make a donation to the church.

"That would be wonderful!" I responded, filling her in on our exact situation. She had no idea that we had recently relocated to a new campus nor that we were in the middle of a vast expansion project. I let her know that we were proceeding by faith. I had no idea whether she intended to send us a few hundred or a few thousand dollars. I was just glad of her interest.

As our conversation drew to a close, I assured the woman, "Please know that anything you send will be deeply appreciated."

"Good!" she replied. "I need to ask you to overnight some documentation about your church. Please make sure it gets to me by tomorrow, since I am meeting with lawyers and accountants to settle a lot of details about the inheritance. As soon as these matters are settled, I'll be sending you a check." I caught my breath when she told me the amount. She wasn't sending a check for $50,000. Nor $100,000. No, she intended to contribute a check in the vicinity of $3,000,000!

Here was a total stranger telling me how God had moved her heart to help us at just the right moment in time. While we chatted some more and then said good-bye, words I had heard before were resounding within me: *Just bless them and trust me to look after you and your needs.*

God's promise applies to each of us today. If you haven't already done so, make it your habit to pray that he will use you to touch the lives of others. As you open your heart to compassion and mercy, God will do exceedingly beyond what you can ever ask or think. As King Solomon experienced so many years ago, God will not only supply the things you ask for, but will also grant you unimaginable blessings. For the Lord is faithful. He does not change. Because he is our Source, we, too, can step out in faith into the realm of breakthrough prayer.

CHAPTER 1: BREAKTHROUGH PRAYER

1. Nicky Cruz's story is told in his book *Run Baby Run* (Plainfield, N.J.: Logos Associates, 1988).
2. David Brainerd's journal, first published in London in 1748, is available today in various editions, both complete and abridged.

CHAPTER 3: CALLING 911

1. Words and music by Dan Dean, Dave Clark, and Don Koch. Copyright © 1995 Dawn Treader Music (SESAC)/ Word Music (a division of Word, Inc.)/First Verse Music/ (ASCAP)/DaySpring Music (a division of Word, Inc.) (BMI).

CHAPTER 12: BREAKTHROUGH JOY

1. *ABC World News Tonight* with Peter Jennings, January 14, 2003.

Fresh Wind, Fresh Fire
What Happens When God's Spirit
Invades the Heart of His People

Jim Cymbala with Dean Merrill

Hardcover: 0-310-21188-3
Softcover: 0-310-25153-2
Abridged Audio Pages® Cassette: 0-310-21199-9
Unabridged Audio Pages® CD: 0-310-23649-5

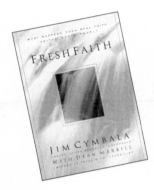

Fresh Faith
What Happens When Real
Faith Ignites God's People

Jim Cymbala with Dean Merrill

Hardcover: 0-310-23007-1
Softcover: 0-310-25155-9
Abridged Audio Pages® Cassette: 0-310-23006-3
Unabridged Audio Pages® CD: 0-310-23639-8

Fresh Power
Experiencing the Vast Resources
of the Spirit of God

Jim Cymbala with Dean Merrill

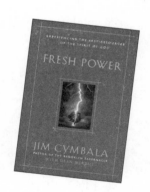

Hardcover: 0-310-23008-X
Softcover: 0-310-25154-0
Abridged Audio Pages® Cassette: 0-310-23476-X
Unabridged Audio Pages® CD: 0-310-24200-2

Pick up a copy today at your favorite bookstore!

ZONDERVAN™

GRAND RAPIDS, MICHIGAN 49530 USA

WWW.ZONDERVAN.COM

The Church God Blesses

Jim Cymbala with Stephen Sorenson

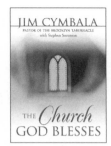

God wants to transform his church into a people of power, joy, and peace. Jim Cymbala reminds us that Christianity is only as strong as the local church and that God wants to bless our churches in ways we can't possibly imagine. It doesn't matter whether a church is alive and growing or barely surviving on life support. God has a plan for it. It doesn't matter whether a church is facing financial challenges, internal divisions, or strife among its leaders. God has a plan for it. God is able to deal with any problem a church will ever face—as long as his people earnestly seek him.

Hardcover: 0-310-24203-7   Unabridged Audio Pages® Cassette: 0-310-24800-0
                                  Unabridged Audio Pages® CD: 0-310-24200-2

God Is Searching for People to Bless!

The Life God Blesses
The Secret of Enjoying God's Favor

Jim Cymbala with Stephen Sorenson

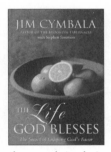

Jim Cymbala believes that God plays "favorites"—that certain people experience his blessings more abundantly than others. Have these people learned a formula or a simple technique that will guarantee his blessing? Or is there something more profound at work in their lives?

In *The Life God Blesses*, Jim Cymbala points out that God is constantly searching for people to bless. He's not looking for men and women with special talents or unusual intelligence or great strength but for those who possess a certain kind of heart. Find out how to have a heart that God cannot resist and you will become a channel of his blessing for your family, your church, and your world.

Hardcover: 0-310-24202-9   Unabridged Audio Pages® Cassette: 0-310-24799-3
                                  Unabridged Audio Pages® CD: 0-310-24798-5

We want to hear from you. Please send your comments about this book to us in care of zreview@zondervan.com. Thank you.

GRAND RAPIDS, MICHIGAN 49530 USA

WWW.ZONDERVAN.COM